What Am I?

WHAT AM I?

Descartes and the Mind-Body Problem

Joseph Almog

OXFORD
UNIVERSITY PRESS

OXFORD
UNIVERSITY PRESS

Oxford University Press, Inc., publishes works that further
Oxford University's objective of excellence
in research, scholarship, and education.

Oxford   New York
Auckland   Cape Town   Dar es Salaam   Hong Kong   Karachi
Kuala Lumpur   Madrid   Melbourne   Mexico City   Nairobi
New Delhi   Shanghai   Taipei   Toronto

With offices in
Argentina   Austria   Brazil   Chile   Czech Republic   France   Greece
Guatemala   Hungary   Italy   Japan   Poland   Portugal   Singapore
South Korea   Switzerland   Thailand   Turkey   Ukraine   Vietnam

Copyright © 2002 by Joseph Almog

First published in 2002 by Oxford University Press, Inc.
198 Madison Avenue, New York, New York 10016

First issued as an Oxford University Press paperback, 2005

www.oup.com

Oxford is a registered trademark of Oxford University Press

All rights reserved. No part of this publication may be reproduced,
stored in a retrieval system, or transmitted, in any form or by any means,
electronic, mechanical, photocopying, recording, or otherwise,
without the prior permission of Oxford University Press.

Library of Congress Cataloging-in-Publication Data
Almog, Joseph.
What am I? : Descartes and the mind-body problem / Joseph Almog.
p. cm.
Includes index.
ISBN-13 978-0-19-514646-2; 978-0-19-517719-0 (pbk.)
ISBN 0-19-514646-8; 0-19-517719-3 (pbk.)
1. Descartes, René, 1596–1650—Contributions in dualist doctrine of
mind and body.   2. Mind and body—History—17th century.   I. Title
B1878.M55 A46 2001
128'.2—dc21   00-067094

1 3 5 7 9 8 6 4 2

Printed in the United States of America
on acid-free paper

Dedicated to my parents, Lea and Joshua

Preface

The title question is vintage Descartes. It makes its debut in his *Meditations on First Philosophy*, on the second page of Meditation II. I refer to it from now on as "the primal question." The text that follows is an attempt to trace Descartes's own answer(s) to this question.[1]

This book has been reconstructed, with minor alterations (footnotes, references, etc.), from a transcript made in a UCLA introductory class, locally known as Philosophy 7, which I have taught every year since coming to UCLA in 1984. The class is given to a large audience of freshmen and sophomores, up to 350 students. Most of them take the class as a "general education" requirement, and it is thus their first, and probably last, exposure to philosophy.

The idea to teach Descartes came to me by accident. In my first year of teaching at UCLA, I had to find some large-audience class to teach. I could not teach ethics or history introductions. By elimination, I was left with Philosophy 7, then a name without any connotation for me. One day I visited the class to get a sense of what it is like to teach it. The teacher, Rogers Albritton, was reading through Meditation II. I was spellbound

---

1. In what follows, I have relied on *The Philosophical Writings of Descartes*, trans. J. Cottingham, R. Stoothoff, and D. Murdoch (Cambridge: Cambridge University Press, 1985), vols. I and II. I refer to the two volumes as CSM I and CSM II. I also refer to *Descartes—Philosophical Letters*, ed. A. Kenny (Minneapolis: University of Minnesota Press, 1970). It is designated in what follows as PL.

and decided to imitate him, which was not very sage on my part, for Albritton is inimitable. But I have found Descartes.

In the first 10 years, the class consisted only of chapter 1 of this book—the proof of the mind-body real distinction. I took myself to be following Descartes's own methodology in Meditation II. Having raised the primal question, he answers it in the next sentence with the phrase "a man." But he goes on to dismiss this primal answer in the following way:

> But what is a man? Shall I say 'rational animal'? No; for then I should inquire what an animal is, what rationality is, and in this way one question would lead me down the slope to harder ones and I do not now have the time to waste on subtleties of this kind. (CSM II, 17)

He soon substitutes the primal question by surrogates—What is Mind? What is Body? It is thus that mind and body "grow capitals." The project as Descartes characterizes it technically is to prove their *real distinction*. The task is to prove that the mind and the body—any old mind and body and never mind whose (A *man's* mind? *This* man's mind?)—are (i) real subjects that (ii) are numerically distinct and (iii) *can exist* without the other. The point of the class for many years was to examine Descartes's proof. After 10 weeks, we would reach a happy end—Descartes's proof vindicated.

The happy end did not tell the full story. I felt that without going back to the primal *question*, we did not come full circle. Stronger yet, as long as we did not consider Descartes's original, quickly dismissed *answer* (i.e., what-I-am is a man, a human being), we would not get a full understanding of Descartes. Most discussions of Descartes and of his progeny—the doctrine of mind-body dualism—started with Mind and Body as the basic notions. They would add as a sort of appendix that somehow, out of these two primal elements, Descartes "composes" (sometimes, "constructs") a full-blooded man.

I knew in my bones that Descartes was not involved in such metaphysical engineering. This was a man who, in the dead of night, bought cadavers in the "street of veal" so that their dissection would teach him about human nature. This was "my" Descartes: a dissector of human beings, in whose nature it is to be first alive and then to turn into such lifeless bodies. But to so ground Descartes in the human condition—the life and death of the human body—ran against much of the atmosphere that radiated from Cartesian studies. I had to keep Descartes out of my sight for some time.

The class, however, had to go on. And so, for a few years I introduced students to the question "What am I?"(or even better: "What makes someone one-of-us?"), using quite a different text—the movie *Blade Runner*, which has its own way of making the question vivid for beginners. But I knew my estrangement from Descartes was only temporary.

It was only around 1996, after teaching Descartes anew in a class in Sweden, that I came to see how he worked his way back to the primal question. I have convinced myself that the key to his methodology lies in his remarks to Princess Elizabeth, especially the last sentence of the following quotation:

> I supposed that your Highness still had in mind the arguments proving the distinction between the soul and the body, and I did not want to ask her to put them away in order to represent herself the notion of the union which everyone has in himself without philosophizing. Everyone feels that he is a single person with both body and thought so related by nature that the thought can move the body and feel the things which happen to it.
> (PL, 142)

Driven by these remarks, I have redesigned the class in recent years. It expounds Descartes as pursuing *the dual key project*: a real distinction in a real man. The challenge to the class in the final exam—a challenge reviewed in the Synopsis, which follows this preface—is to evaluate whether the real distinction argument has been successfully embedded in a framework that respects the integrity of the man as a real subject.

Running this class for more than 15 years led me to accumulate many debts. I am grateful to the philosophy department of UCLA and to the university as a whole for supporting such an "exotic" general education course. In public education, where there is a will, there is a way.

I am grateful to many past and present colleagues for discussions of this class and related metaphysical issues: Tyler Burge, Keith Donnellan, Kit Fine, Barbara Herman, Tony Martin, the late Warren Quinn, Abe Roth, Seana Shiffrin, Sean Kelsey, and Mike Thau. My fellow historians John Carriero and Calvin Normore have given this book a most thorough reading despite the fact that its author must have seemed to them an accidental tourist in the land of Descartes studies. I have learned much about the mind-body union from interacting in Vancouver with Catherine Wilson and in Uppsala with Lilli Alanen. This class also owes much to extremely dedicated teaching assistants who struggled in creative ways to make the material sensible to students: Andrew Hsu, Michael Thompson, Torin Alter, Keith Kaiser, Erin Eaker, and Dominik Sklenar. Finally, throughout the process, I found Peter Ohlin of Oxford University Press a deft and supportive editor.

The greatest influence over my metaphysical formation, if anything could be so called, has come from three philosophers: the inspiring pedagogue Rogers Albritton; Saul Kripke in his book *Naming and Necessity*, a sort of modern-day *Meditations*, whose luminous language is responsible for the way we do metaphysics (and that, in this positivist age, we do it at all); finally, there are the daily interactions, for two decades, with my teacher, David Kaplan.

The last word before the reader confronts the text proper regards the fundamental *limits* of the present book. Though I enjoyed the years of teaching Descartes and the mind-body problem, I feel something is amiss with my work on both.

Regarding Descartes, my readings of his work are far from "complete." For one example, the leading interpretation I offer in chapters 2 and 3, what I call *integrative dualism*, ignores

Descartes's seeming promise to leave room for the immortality of the soul. For another such example, many of my historian friends have pushed me to trace the thread between Descartes and his medieval predecessors. Some (not the same) have argued I should connect him with his rationalist successors, e.g., Kant. Now, at times, Descartes does use the metaphysical language of the medievals. Also, Descartes does have moods in which he speaks in a very intellectualized, abstract way about our ideas and our reason. But what always struck me is how perceptual, indeed *sensuous*, a philosopher he is. His explanations of the workings of human beings are strikingly graphic, be they of the circulatory system and the pineal gland or be they, as in his *Passions of the Soul*, of emotional states such as love and admiration. Throughout, I view him like a gardener touching his beloved flowers delicately, as he sketches them on a piece of paper. With this picture in mind, I have elected to keep Descartes a philosopher-by-nose rather than a late medievalist or an early rationalist. I am sure this makes the Descartes that follows substantially incomplete.

What applies to the Descartes that follows applies even more so to what I say about the mind-body problem in general. By this last, I refer to a casting of the problem in modern (twenty-first century) terms, using concepts from the philosophy of language, (modal) logic and other such "technology." The incompleteness runs deeper here. There is on the one hand a sense of local progress on this or that "technical issue." But it is coupled with a deeper feeling of not getting to the bottom of the real problem. I track a like-minded recognition of this kind of "technical sublimation" in the writings of Tom Nagel. Without drafting his writings to support the present discomfort, let me explain my own reservations.

By "local progress" on technical issues, I mean something like this. In research lectures (though not in the aforementioned classes), I project some ideas from what I call Descartes's integrative dualism to the modern version of the dispute between materialists and neo-Cartesian dualists, of whom I take Saul

Kripke to be the leading expounder. It is thus that I have come to think, perhaps against Kripke, that we need not assert the *real possibility* of mentality (say, my state of pain) without a brain state, or the possibility of a brain state (say, the firing of such and such brain fibers) without the corresponding mental state of pain. I, for one, would see the two—the physical and mental (type of) states—as bound by modal necessity; stronger yet, I see them as interconnected by *their very nature*. Related to this is the sense I express in chapter 3 that there is no ground under the various brain-body-swap scenarios fantasized about in the contemporary personal identity literature. Nor do I see critics of materialism (like myself) needed to accept the possibility of so-called zombies (beings with our kind of physical brain structure but no mental experiences). All of these imagined possibilities are illusory and not required in a defense of (i) the numerical distinctness of the mind (and its states) from the body (and its states) and of (ii) what I describe in the book as the *categorical* difference of matters physical (or physical-functional) from any thing mental.

So much I feel I can argue for. Nonetheless, there remains the abovementioned *malaise*. I do not think that such local improvements have provided me with a clear *language* with which to teach what is the mind-body *problem*. The substance language of Descartes—do we have here one or two things (subjects, substances)?—is one philosophical language we all use to talk about the problem; the modern reference to mental and physical *properties* (or for that matter, kinds of states) is another such language. I believe that within these languages, we can make useful moves, ascertain what premises need to be asserted by a given position, what items are identical with what, and what depends on what. All of this leaves the discomfort where it was, the feeling that these "technical" philosophical languages do not get to the bottom of the problem. I often say to the students: many complain that when it comes to the mind-body problem, we have a fundamental question and no clear answers;

for me, it is the other way round: we have many clear answers but no fundamental question.

Perhaps we are overly wedded to the standard philosophical languages. At one point in his correspondence with Princess Elizabeth, Descartes, after he himself so ingeniously used the standard philosophical languages of his time, says to her that to understand the mind-body union, one needs to bracket away metaphysical analysis and fall back on "ordinary life and conversation." Well, I tried. Such is the aforementioned graphic language of the movie *Blade Runner*. Recently, I have so deployed in teaching the language of an imaginative novel, *The Golden Compass* (by Philip Pullman). The author there connects in a most beguiling way each person—seemingly a kind-mate of you and me—with what he calls his (her) *daemon*. Such graphic aids are invaluable but one still feels the problem has not been *articulated*.

The philosopher by nose he was, I do think that Descartes smelled things right—the insight that is needed will come not from, but in spite of, technical philosophical languages, by attending to our "ordinary life and conversation." At this time, I don't know how to do it.

Saint Jean Du Gard, France   J. A.
July 2000

Contents

Synopsis: The Project and the Challenge, xvii

1. The Real Distinction, 3
   1.1. The Basis for the Real Distinction, 3
   1.2. What Is in a Real Distinction?, 4
   1.3. Conceivability, Possibility, Whatness, 5
   1.4. The Argument from Possibility—Descartes vs. Arnauld, 14
   1.5. The Primacy of Whatness, 23
   1.6. Appendix: Conceivability—Does Epistemology Precede Metaphysics?, 42

2. Integrative Dualism, 59
   2.1. The Prove Too Much/Prove Too Little Dilemma, 59
   2.2. Separatist Dualism: Four Basic Annotations, 61
   2.3. Integrative Dualism: The Quest for Symmetry, 71
   2.4. Subjects in Time: Two Cartesian Frameworks, 81

3. The Real Man, 99
   3.1. The Real Distinction Reviewed, 99
   3.2. The Primal Question and the Primal Answer, 115

Index, 125

Synopsis: The Project and the Challenge

Descartes's dual key project targets two objectives. The first is the separation of the human mind and body, the second their integration into a human being. The demands—separation yet integration—seem to make the project impossible. As often, Descartes himself best articulates the project and the challenge facing it. In his fourth replies, his response to Arnauld, he formulates his project (the dual key project) and the challenge—*the prove too much/prove too little dilemma*:

> Nor do I see why this argument "proves too much." For the fact that one thing can be separated from another by the power of God is the very least that can be asserted in order to establish that there is a real distinction between the two. Also, I thought I was very careful to guard against anyone inferring from this that man was simply "a soul which makes use of a body." ... Now someone who says that a man's arm is a substance that's really distinct from the rest of his body does not thereby deny that the arm belongs to the nature of the whole man ... nor do think I proved too little in saying that the mind is substantially united with the body, since that substantial union does not prevent our having a clear and distinct concept of the mind on its own, as a complete thing. (CSM II, 160)

Let me put the dilemma in my own words. We might be so successful at separating mind and body that when we put them together again to form a single man, we no longer get a real, natural unity—a full-blooded human subject—but what Descartes calls a mere "unity of composition," an artificial compound. Thus, we have the "prove too much" horn. To amend things, we might start by carefully protecting the primality of the full human being. But then whatever separation-in-our-conception we grant mind and body, it is not enough to establish them, our conception aside, as distinct, complete subjects, each of which can exist without the other. Thus we have the "prove too little" horn of the dilemma.[1]

We shall follow Descartes's two-stage defusing of the prove too much/prove too little dilemma. Chapter 1 will discuss his argument for the real distinction, and chapter 2 will expound his way of integrating mind and body into a single real man. By this point, we will evaluate how Descartes fares vis-à-vis the dilemma.

I do not provide such a resolution. I doubt, in general, the feasibility of quests for "the one and only interpretation," even more with so subtle a thinker as Descartes, ever the master of nuances, depending on who his interlocutor is. More instructive in my view is to recognize that various forms of dualism may be distilled from Descartes's texts. It is then interesting to separate the questions for each framework and see how, within a given framework, an outstanding puzzle is worked out.

To reiterate: In the following text I have no ambition to uproot other interpretations in order to leave room for this one orchid—the "real" Descartes. I would rather let a couple of such flowers—and more—bloom.

---

1. I should say that in teaching this critical dilemma-setting paragraph, I often suggest replacing, in the example, the arm by the brain. There is then a much better intuitive sense to the claim that though both items are complete subjects, they existentially depend—by their very nature—on each other.

What Am I?

ONE

The Real Distinction

1.1. The Basis for the Real Distinction

In a letter written on January 19, 1642, to Father Gibieuf, Descartes says:

> The idea of a substance with its extension and shape is a complete idea because I can conceive it alone and deny of it everything else of which I have an idea. Now it seems to me very clear that the idea of a thinking substance is complete in this sense, and that I have in mind no other idea which is prior to it and joined to it in such a way that I cannot think of the two together while denying the one of the other. (PL, 24)

A similar observation about the completeness of the idea of his mind recurs in Descartes's reply to what strikes me as the most penetrating objection made to him, Arnauld's (the fourth) objection. In what follows, I try my hand at a defense of Descartes's proof by reviewing his back-and-forth exchange with Arnauld. My sense is that if Descartes can work his way out of Arnauld's objection, he is on the homestretch.[1]

---

1. The readings I take to be relevant to this issue and which are referred to in detail below are the exchange with Arnauld over "complete ideas" in the fourth replies (CSM II, 156–160), related remarks to Caterus in the first replies (CSM II, 85–86), and the letters to Mesland (May 2, 1644, PL, 152) and Gibieuf (PL, 24).

1.2. What Is in a Real Distinction?

When I speak of "the real distinction of mind and body," we must keep in mind two simple observations. The first concerns the nature of the intended relation-real distinction; the second, the nature of the purported relata.

Concerning the first distinction and following Descartes, I will gloss "x and y are really distinct" as "x and y are substances and x and y can exist without each other." In this gloss, "without each other" will be taken "weakly"; that is, it is enough that at least one of x and y can exist without the other. What is more, we need to be intentionally primitive about the "can" in "can exist without the other." Today many readings offer very sophisticated senses of this "can." Reference is made to "epistemic," "logical," and "metaphysical" brands of possibility, as if such technical notions were as old as the hills; the language of "possible worlds" is invoked, and it is said that "there is some possible world where the mind exists without the body." More generally, much of the sophistication from modern studies of modal logic and its model theory (semantics) shows in analyses of Descartes.

I want us to regain our innocence. Descartes's "can" is just the "can" of the vernacular. Whether it means an "epistemic can," a "modal can," or yet a third, hitherto undelineated "can" is an open question. We should not prejudge the force of Descartes's "can" by infusing sophisticated modern readings.

Second, I now come to the nature of the relata involved. In many discussions of Descartes's real distinction proof—his own Meditation VI discussion is a paradigm in this respect (CSM I, 56)—there is a gap in proving that (i) his mind and body are really distinct and (ii) he and his body (in his mouth: I and my body) are really distinct. Our question in chapter 1 is this: Are Descartes's mind (DM) and Descartes's body (DB) really distinct? The question about the man Descartes or, more neutrally, the referent of his "I"—whether it (he) is distinct from DB—is left for chapter 2.

1.3. Conceivability, Possibility, Whatness

Existentially Separatist Arguments

There are at least three arguments of Descartes that we shall be looking at—the argument from *conceivability*, the argument from *possibility*, and the argument from *whatness*. The three share a certain form. Each provides (i) a *numerical discernibility* argument and (ii) an *existential discernibility* argument. By (i) I mean that the argument isolates some genuine property of individuals F—the discerning property—and states: The mind bears F but the body does not. Using logic, the argument applies Leibniz's principle of *distinctness of discernibles*: Individuals discernible by any genuine property F are numerically distinct individuals. It is concluded that the mind is numerically distinct from the body; they make two distinct subjects.

In addition, all three arguments have a particular *way*—the way of existential separation—of ascertaining the numerical distinction. Each asserts that the mind can exist without the body. This last claim is found by analyzing the preceding premises: The mind bears property F but the body does not. Shortly we shall discuss how exactly one "gets" existential separability from the discerning property F. Sometimes F wears the existential separability on its sleeves; sometimes more analysis is called for to isolate it. But for the moment let us call arguments that secure both numerical and existential discernibility *existentially separatist* arguments.

In a slightly more canonical form, our three arguments are as follows:

(1) DM bears F.

(2) It is not the case that DB bears F.

Now, by the distinctness of discernibles:

(3) DM ≠ DB.

It is then added that given the meaning of the discerning feature *F*, premise (1) gives us further:

(4) DM can exist without DB.

It is time to verify how this basic mold shows up in the three Cartesian arguments.

The Argument from Conceivability

In the argument from conceivability, the discerning property *F* is as follows: "Conceivably exists without DB" (or stronger yet, "without any body whatsoever"). We get

(1C) DM conceivably exists without DB.

(2C) It is not the case that DB conceivably exists without DB.

Hence,

(3C) DM ≠ DB.

This takes care of the numerical distinction. But where are we to get the real distinction of DM and DB? It is suggested that the truth of (1C) provides a locus—a scenario in our head—in which DM can exist without DB. We may thus assert, "in a conceived story" sense of "can," that

(4C) DM can exist without DB.

The Argument from Possibility

In the argument from possibility, the discerning property is "possibly exists without DB," that is, has the real possibility of existing without DB. We then get

(1P) DM possibly exists without DB.

(2P) It is not the case that DB possibly exists without DB.

Hence,

(3P) DM ≠ DB.

It is now argued that (1P) directly gives us

(4P) DM can exist without DB.

The Argument from Whatness

In the argument from whatness, the target property F relies on the notion of the kind of thing DM is, that is, the nature of DM or what-DM-is. I use this vocabulary to formulate F as "by whatness thinking":

(1W) DM is *by whatness thinking*.

(2W) It is not the case that DB is *by whatness thinking*.

(3W) DM ≠ DB.

The premises of the whatness argument are much more prudent. Indeed, its very point is to proceed from a denial of the preceding possibility argument: Though DM and DB may of necessity coexist (in union), they are nonetheless ascertainable as numerically distinct. So unlike the first two arguments, the whatness argument does not assert directly the existential separability of DM and DB. There thus remains the question of whether DM and DB are not only numerically but also really distinct, that is, existentially separable. Establishing such existential separation will not be as easy as it was before; this is, after all, the virtue of the present argument. But those accustomed to witnessing a numerical distinction by existential separability will insist on posing the following question: Is there no way to save, as Descartes wanted, a logically objective sense of "can" according to which DM can exist without DB? The question calls for some careful discussion.

THE QUEST FOR WHATNESS AND
COHERENT STORIES

We are walking a tightrope here. The logically objective sense of "can" that we are looking for must be weaker than a real possibility yet stronger than a merely "epistemic can": "For all the information available to DM that is immuned to Cartesian doubt, DM may exist without DB." To get such a weaker than real possibility yet objective existential separation, we may argue as follows.

The claim that what-x-is is an F is equivalent to this proposition: It is not logically consistent with what x is that x is not F. We may now add this: To every such consistency claim, there is a corresponding "coherent story" (model) about x. The intended idea is that there may be consistent stories about x that nonetheless are not genuine possibilities for x. Our quest is for a story that is logically consistent with what DM is but one that is subtracting DB.

Consider all the coherent stories about DM. Either DB is present in them all or it is not. If it is not present in at least one of them, we are done—DM can exist without DB. But what if, story by story, we find that whenever DM is present, DB is?

At this juncture, readers of Descartes's Meditation II may well be thinking of a variety of growingly strong premises, all of which I call *subtraction principles*. The weakest is this:

(S1)   Let the specification of what-x-is, for example, an F, *not* involve some particular subject y; also, what-y-is is *not* an *F*; then, there exists a coherent story where *x* exists but *y* does not.

Some such premise might rid DM of the specific body DB it is in union with, while still demanding that every coherent story about DM makes it embodied. This kind of argument is very popular with theories of personal identity that come from John Locke and are embraced by many in our time. We shall have the occasion to dwell on such theories later. Such (neo-)Lockean theories sustain the sense of a story or "case" about DM without DB.

A principle stronger than (S1) and deniable by the neo-Lockean tradition seems extractible from Descartes:

(S2) Let the specification of what-*x*-is, for example, an *F*, *not* involve any object of another kind (whatness) *G*; then, there exists a coherent story where *x* exists but no *G* objects do.

According to this principle, there exists a coherent story with a totally disembodied DM. Both (S1) and (S2) assume that no reference to extendedness or materiality has been made in specifying what DM is ("a thinking thing").

Finally, some read Meditation II as providing a scenario in which Descartes's mind is all by itself. They point to the coherence of the supposition that an evil genius has been feeding Descartes's mind illusions about his body, other men, and the rest of the external world. The coherence of such a story would provide the basis of yet a stronger principle, a superposition of the foregoing two:

(S3) Let the specification of what-*x*-is, for example, an *F*, *not* involve any specific object *y* and any other kind (whatness) of objects *G*; then there exists a coherent story where *x* exists but (i) no *G* objects exist and (ii) *y* does not exist.

According to (S3), there is a coherent story about DM in which nothing but it (and the creator of all things) exists, not even other soul mates, that is, other thinking things.

To reiterate, none of the above (S1)–(S3) arguments may represent a genuine possibility for DM. But, by the lights of Meditation II, each submits a coherent story, one witnessing what strictly belongs in DM's nature; what does not belong may be coherently subtracted. Such subtractive stories, weak or strong, justify our drawing from the whatness argument the further result of a real distinction:

(4W)   DM can exists without DB.

Descartes's Projection Method

The arguments from conceivability, possibility, and whatness seem autonomous, and we can consider the merits of each separately. A modern eye, trained in the metaphysics of possibility and essence (whatness), will certainly take the arguments from possibility and whatness as standing on their own. Thus, many modern metaphysicians have been happy to assert that (i) Richard Nixon might have lost the 1968 elections; (ii) it is necessary, though not pertaining to what he is, that Nixon was the *actual* winner in 1968; and (iii) his being human does pertain to what he is. These truths have been standardly submitted by modern metaphysicians without an accompanying theory of how we *know* them to be true. I am surely one such "modern."

However, in the context of Descartes's arguments, it is clear, most of the time, that this is not the order of ideas (chapter 2 will stress the few times when this is not so clear). In a natural first reading of Descartes, the argument from conceivability is the fundamental one, serving as the basis for the remaining two. Driven by this fact about Descartes's affinities, we focus here on the possible justification of his conceivability argument. As mentioned, this goes against my metaphysical grain. Nonetheless, I feel that the focus on conceivability has its benefits, in addition to the already mentioned virtue of staying close to Descartes. We are thus forced to ponder this intriguing question: What makes conceivability such a metaphysically (i) sound and (ii) complete tracking method?[2]

As emphasized, Descartes's starting point is his argument from conceivability. The two remaining arguments are projections from conceivability to something more objective, something that is meant to be conceivability free. In the first projection, we are finding a real possibility for DM. In the second, we are finding what is logically consistent with what DM is, what is not excluded by its objective essence. Either way, our conceivability experiments have been left behind. We now have the objectual targets proper—DM and DB. What discerns them is something in their own objective (i) potentialities and/or (ii) essence (the kind of thing they are).

Common to both projections is the following two-step mold, what I'd like to call Descartes's basic *projection mold*. Step 1 starts with some direct data, and so I call it *data articulation*. We consider what we can conceive of DM and of DB. The results are available to us—to our intellect—directly; furthermore, the results are known to us with supreme certainty.

Given this data articulation, we are ready to move on to step 2, the projection step. Sometimes, our objective is the projection of a real possibility of DM without DB. We rely then on the following scheme:

(Real possibility projection) Whatever is (clearly, distinctly and completely) conceivable about a given subject x is really possible for x.

---

2. The notions of a sound and complete tracking method will be introduced in detail later; see 1.6. At this stage, it is enough to say that by the metaphysical *soundness* of the method, I mean that what is conceivable about x is indeed possible for x (consistent with its nature). By *completeness*, I mean the converse: If something is possible for x (consistent with x's nature), then it is conceivable about it; that is, conceivability about x completely exhausts what is possible for x (consistent with its nature).

Alternatively, our target may be to establish the weaker claim, that whether it is really possible or not, it is logically consistent with DM's essence—being a thinking thing—that it exists without DB, indeed without any extended thing around. To so project, we call on this scheme:

> (Coherent story projection) Whatever is (clearly, distinctly and completely) conceivable about a subject x is logically consistent with what it is and attributable to x in a coherent story (model) about it.

Given the soundness of such projections, we are given a real possibility, or a coherent story, in which (i) DM exists and DB does not. It follows that (ii) in that possibility (coherent story) DM is distinct from DB. But then it follows that (iii), in reality, DM is numerically distinct from DB.[3]

However, by this very argument, DM is not only distinct in reality from DB but also "really distinct"—in the technical sense—from it: It can exist without it. The "can" may mean either "in a real possibility" or merely "in a coherent story," depending on which argument has been followed.

---

3. This last step, from distinctness in a possibility (coherent story) to distinctness in reality, is due to the *logical* stability of identity and distinctness relations: If x is (not) identical to y, then in all possibilities (coherent stories) x is (not) identical to y. Many in the first half of the twentieth century, doubted these principles, because they confused the coincidence of two individual concepts (presentations of individuals in our thinking) with the relation of objectual identity between the individuals proper. Others have doubted the principles because they confused the objectual relation with its linguistic representation: $a = b$ sentences with proper names a and b. In contrast, Descartes and Arnauld—very much like modern (modal) logicians—were crystal clear about the logic of identity and assumed the stability principles as a matter of course. They did not confuse the relation proper with how we present it to ourselves, in thought or in language. With Descartes and Arnauld, we assume the logical principles throughout this work. The emphasis on the distinction between representations of identity and the objectual relation will concern us later in this chapter, in the extended discussion of conceivability, de dicto, and de re.

In reconstructing Descartes's order of argument, we first have to take notice of the primacy of the conceivability argument. Descartes abides by a distinctive flow diagram:

Conceivability ———⟶ possibility (coherent story)
———⟶ reality

Second, in contrast, the most ubiquitous projective argument considered by critics of Descartes—for example, Arnauld in the fourth objections—is the possibility argument. The objections are formulated against it. It is only in the subsequent Cartesian reply that the attenuated (weaker and more sophisticated) projective argument from whatness and coherent separation emerges. In this sense, the possibility argument is the "first blush" projection argument, and the whatness and coherent separation argument is a subsequent correction; that is, when it is realized, we can obtain our desired real distinction from weaker premises.

In the reconstruction below, I will follow the dynamics of the Descartes-Arnauld exchanges. We shall examine first the possibility argument, look at Arnauld's objection to it, and then move to Descartes's repartee. This will lead us to Descartes's argument from whatness and coherent separation.[4]

---

4. It may seem that we have ignored, on behalf of Descartes, an obvious third path. Why not use the argument from conceivability without any projection, either of possibility or coherent separation? After all, if DM has a property—conceivable without DB—that DB lacks, by Leibniz's law (distinctness of discernibles), it seems that the game is over, that DM and DB are numerically distinct. And it may be claimed that we have here a real distinction—we *can* conceive of DM without DB. Thus, in this sense of "can"—can in the understanding—DM can exist without DB. What, if anything, is wrong with such a direct, projection-free argument? Perhaps nothing. The fact remains that Descartes (and Arnauld) fixed on projection arguments. I, a reconstructor of both, will follow them. By the time we have distilled the most defensible of the projection arguments—the end of chapter 1—I shall return to the theme of an altogether projection-free argument and ask (i) has it been followed by Descartes and (ii) could it justify the real distinction?

1.4. The Argument from Possibility—
Descartes vs. Arnauld

We need to fix on the sense of possibility intended in the argument. The possibility targeted is meant to be real. This is in contrast to the merely formal or combinatorial possibilities that were to be so attractive subsequently to Hume and more modern philosophers (most of whom I regard as skeptical about real possibility). In the merely formal sense, any combinatorial possibility is a possibility. Thus consider Princess Elizabeth. Some pertinent facts about her are these: What she was—the kind of being she was—was a human being; she lived in the seventeenth century; she was not the daughter of Pablo Picasso and Lana Turner. Also, she was an astute mathematician, an intriguing correspondent, and interested in the passions.

The combinatorialist sees these traits as all of a kind when it comes to delineating what is and is not possible for the princess. It is possible that she would not be good in mathematics and not care about the passions. But it is equally possible that she would live in our time or Aristotle's; be the daughter of Picasso; and still in the same breath, be a flower, a river, or a book about the passions. All are possibilities for Elizabeth—as indeed for any other object—because none are formally contradictory. The combination of this bare subject—Elizabeth—with any of the properties does not produce a formal, logical contradiction. In the same vein, classed as impossible are only her being identical to Descartes (assuming identity belongs in logic), her being both a flower and not a flower, and perhaps her being both married and single.

The Descartes-Arnauld idea of possibility is not the combinatorialist idea. Some will insist that both Descartes and Arnauld allude, sometimes, to "what God can create (do)." Is this not a step away from "real possibility" and toward more extraordinary possibilities? Perhaps so. But Arnauld would not allow God to create a right triangle that does not abide by Pythagoras' theorem, make the sum of 5 and 7 not be 12, make a body that is not extended, and so on. Alas, Descartes, though not in his work on mind and body, sometimes seems to allow God to create the uncreatable (the "truth" that 5 and 7 make 13). I ignore here such uses of "creativity" and "possibility."

Both Descartes and Arnauld use a nonformalist, real-individual-bound idea of possibility, possibilities determined by the essence of the subject *for* whom (which) they are possibilities. Both Descartes and Arnauld abide by the principle of *whatness closure*:

(WC) If F pertains to what x is, then F is modally necessary for x.

Already (WC) excludes much of the combinatorialist creation of possibilities cut from whole cloth. What the princess is is a human being, and what the Loire is is a river. Consequently, she cannot be a water pathway leading the liquid from the Massif Central to the Atlantic. And it—the river—cannot be a princess or a philosopher or a passions bearer.

Of course, some delicate issues remain. One is this: Do we have the converse of (WC), that is,

(CWC) If F is modally necessary for x, F pertains to what x is.

Equivalently, if F does *not* pertain to x's whatness, does it follow that it is really possible for x to be not-F? This question will reverberate through the Arnauld-Descartes exchanges as we move from the possibility argument to the coherent separation argument. But whatever refinements await us, it is fair to say that Descartes and Arnauld operate through and through with a nonformalist, genuinely de-subject (what technical philosophy would term *de re*) notion of real possibility. Indeed, the objection Arnauld is about to raise against Descartes and Descartes's response will convince us that both assume a most robust idea of possibility-for-a-subject.[5]

---

5. Sophisticated readers often ask whether the Descartes-Arnauld notion of possibility corresponds to the modern idea—derived from Saul Kripke—that is often called metaphysical possibility or, as I prefer to put it, follow-

The possibility argument targets a real possibility for Descartes's mind: Just as it might have had other intellectual accidents—have had different desires and thoughts—it might have existed without any attachment to this body DB; indeed, it might have existed without DB existing at all; stronger yet, it might have existed without any (human) body in existence.

Possibilities galore, muses Arnauld in the beginning of his fourth objections. But where from? Ascribed on what grounds?

Descartes's answer is that they are all conceivable of DM. But "conceivable" how? Remembering our opening quotation from the letter to Gibieuf; we know that Descartes has some important qualifications—adverbs of manner—to add here. He targets a conception that is clear and distinct and, most critical, complete about the subject. Still, qualifications and all, his defense is this: The foregoing ascriptions of real possibility are justified once they appear to us as conceivable. It is this justification that Arnauld finds flawed.

Arnauld's Objection

In speaking of Arnauld's objection, we must separate the *case* Arnauld presents from the *theoretical* conclusions (objections) one may base on it. The case is one; the theoretical conclusions it may lead to are many. The case runs like this:

---

ing Kripke's own use, "possibility tout court." Here we encounter one of the advantages of lecturing about Descartes to immaculate beginners; they do not ask questions of this kind. More seriously, I find it hard to make such comparisons. The examples used by Descartes and Arnauld concern mathematics. In contrast, a favorite stock of examples in our age concerns the natural sciences (e.g., water is made in part of oxygen; gold is an atomic element; etc.). Nonetheless, I happen to believe that the modern notion of Kripke is more continuous with the Descartes-Arnauld discussion than the 300-year gap might lead us to think. Still, in what follows I make an effort not to indulge in time travel from Descartes's period to ours. Our discussion—inevitably one run by a contemporary mind shaped by contemporary texts—aims at understanding Descartes's text in his own terms.

Suppose that someone knows for certain that the angle
in a semi circle is a right angle and hence that the triangle formed by this angle and the diameter of the circle is
right angled. In spite of this he may doubt, or not yet
grasped for certain, that the square on the hypotenuse is
equal to the squares on the two sides; indeed he may
even deny this if he is misled by some fallacy. (CSM II,
141–142)

Since so much concerns Arnauld's right triangle, let us call
it T, conceived without the Pythagorean property, in short, P.
In analogy to the seeming possibility of supposing T without
P, Arnauld would like us to consider the seeming possibility of
supposing my mind without my body:

But someone might call this minor premise into doubt
and maintain that the conception you have of yourself
when you conceive of yourself as thinking, non extended, thing is an inadequate one ... how is my perception of the nature of my mind any clearer than his perception of the nature of the triangle? ... Although I
clearly and distinctly know my nature to be something
that thinks, may I, too, not perhaps be wrong in thinking that nothing else belongs to my nature apart from
the fact that I am thinking thing? Perhaps the fact that I
am an extended thing may also belong to my nature.
(CSM II, 141–143)

These are Arnauld's actual words. How are we to understand
the theoretical bite of his example? What, if anything, does it
show?

The First Reaction: The Primacy
of Possibility

What is Arnauld's own reaction? Arnauld prizes above all the
possibility-projection schema—whatever is really conceivable is

really possible. And he is wedded to it not because he views possibility facts as based on conceivability facts. Quite the opposite: Arnauld noticed, very cunningly, indeed, that quite apart from any conceivability test, it is a *brute fact* that

(A) It is not possible for triangle T to exist without P.

This much obtains not because we try to *conceive* of T without P and fail. Rather, altogether before any use of conceivability, we are given that if T actually bears P, it necessarily bears P. Admittedly, not every property of T allows for such "necessitation"; for example, T has the property of being Arnauld's favorite figure, in short, Q. But it is not necessary that T bears Q; Arnauld may have been fonder of squares. So, some properties of T—perhaps those expressing mathematical facts—are necessitation-receptive, some are not, and all of this does not depend on what we may or may not be able to conceive.

Very well then: It is impossible for T to exist without P. Arnauld now argues that it is not *really conceivable* of T that it is without P. Here Arnauld asserts that what is not really possible is not really conceivable. In other words, he asserts the possibility projection scheme—whatever is really conceivable is really possible.

What Arnauld rejects is rather:

(Real conceivability projection) What we seem to conceive of x, we really conceive of x.

This, the epistemic transparency of conceivability data, is Descartes's starting point: It could not turn out that it seemed to me that I conceived—with the pertinent adverbial qualifications—of something but I really failed. This much could happen with more external verbs of activity like "touch" or perhaps even "see." I may seem to touch and even see the singer Madonna, but this will not make it a real touching or seeing of her. But if I seem to conceive of Madonna, I, *eo ipso*, really do conceive of her. There can be no gap between seeming to conceive and succeeding in doing so.

The epistemic transparency made conceivability an attractive starting point for Descartes, and it is exactly what Arnauld denies him. Modern examples—exploiting empirically grounded necessities—have pushed this point further than Arnauld did. Thus, I may seem to be able to conceive of water on a planet where there is no oxygen. I envision a liquid that is raining from the sky, running in rivers, tasting like water, and so on. But, many will retort, I have not really conceived of water on this planet. There is no conceiving of water without the conceiving of H_2O; this is simply what water is.

So, we must redescribe our activity. What I have done really is to conceive of some water look-alike, or the-seeming-of-water. Next, I have misdescribed my act as the real conceiving of water, as the conceiving of real water.[6]

Here, of course, the gap between seeming and being is more obvious. The essential fact about water—it is H_2O—is only empirically given; men in Descartes's time did not know it at all (and were surely already thinking about water). In Arnauld's case, we are concerned with mathematical facts that are reputedly all knowable a priori; at any rate, the Pythagorean property was surely so known by mathematicians for ages. Thus, the gap seems harder to generate. Nonetheless, Arnauld insists, we may seem to think about a mathematical object (or kind of object) and be unaware of its full list of necessary properties; stronger yet, we may be aware of the property (we think about and consider the applicability of the property) and consciously deny it.

Extended to the case of the mind, Arnauld's point would come to this: I may very well conceive of my mind—for that matter, our kind of mind—and apply to this subject a certain specific property: its need for an underlying body. We suppose

---

6. This way of explaining the gap between seeming and real conceivability is discussed in some detail in the appendix I.6, page 42.

now that, in fact, it turns out that it is not merely actually true that my mind is connected to a (this) body but also that of necessity it is so connected. If so, I stand corrected in my conceivability claim. I have not really conceived of my mind in this exercise; I have merely conceived of a mind, or of an epistemically equivalent subject that from the inside is indistinguishable from my (our kind of) mind. Of that item, I have conceived—really conceived—that it exists without bodily connection. This does not show that I can so conceive of my (our kind of) mind. All in all, concludes Arnauld, DM and DB may well be necessarily connected. They may or may not be two items (this much is left open). But there is no real possibility of DM without DB. In this sense of "can," there is no real distinction between DM and DB. Descartes refuted.

The Second Reaction: The Primacy of Conceivability

Arnauld's reaction to his own case is based on the idea that possibility precedes conceivability. In assessing the question of whether it is conceivable that water exists without oxygen or T is conceivable without bearing property P, we are already given the fact that these eventualities are not possible. This much is not possible independently of any conceivability fact.

An opposite reaction to Arnauld's case is driven by an opposite doctrine, *the primacy of conceivability*. Conceivability facts, what is and is not conceivable, are determined prior to and independently of the determination of what is possible.

Now, a strong form of this doctrine proposes that conceivability facts *determine* possibility facts. But this strong form—the metaphysical subordination of possibility to conceivability—is not the motivation of our presently examined response to Arnauld's case. The response is rather driven by a concern about *epistemology*—the wish to preserve, with Descartes, the *epistemic transparency* of conceivability claims. In this line of thought, conceivability is thus intrinsically different from sense perception; in turn, it is intrinsically different from any notion of imagination based on such perception. When I claim that I see Madonna in front of me, I know that I may turn out to be wrong. Prior facts about the external world may give the lie to my claim, and twice over: There may be no such item at all (I hallucinate) or I am getting the object in front of me wrong (it is a look-alike and not Madonna that I am seeing). No such openness to correction by antecedent facts governs conceivability claims: If I seem to conceive of Madonna, I really do. In this respect, "conceive" operates like "seem to see" rather than "see."

This view sacrifices the reliability of conceivability as a guide to possibility only to regain the reliability of our own self-ascriptions of what we conceive. Regarding Arnauld's triangle, this view proposes that we did manage to conceive T without P (though it is not possible for T to exist P-less); furthermore, we do conceive of water even if we make it—in the story—oxygenless; and we may well conceive of Elizabeth even if we misplace her in time, flouting a necessary truth, and place her in the eighteenth century. In the mind-body case, the response asserts that we are successful in conceiving the mind without any body on hand, even if it turned out to be impossible for the mind to exist without (this specific) embodiment. The question of whether we manage to conceive of the mind-bearing property F is simply prior to the question of whether that mind could have really been F. If it could not, fine: We have already conceived of it as bearing F.

In sum, the present response suggests that we seem to conceive of DM without DB; thus, we really do. In our conception (or "in the understanding"), DM is distinct from DB. We would now like to conclude as follows: and so, in reality, DM is distinct from DB. What is needed for this last step is a certain kind of conceivability-reflecting-reality projection principle.

Exactly what kind of principle? A general reality-projection principle cannot be correct. Just because I conceive of you on the beach in Rio does not make you be there. But there may be a restricted class of logically privileged relations for which the passage from mere conception to reality is defensible. This would be the case not because the conceiving *makes* reality be its way. Quite the opposite: I can succeed in conceiving of a certain—logically privileged kind of—eventuality only *because* reality is this way. For example, it is only because in reality DM is distinct from DB that I can conceive of them apart. Thus, to get the intended reading of the principle—what fixes what—we should read it contrapositively: If in reality the distinctness does not obtain, it can not obtain in the understanding either. This is why I call the projection schema *the reflection (of reality) principle*.

For the reflection principle to work, we need something more than a restriction to logically privileged relations; we need restrictions on the manner in which the *relata*—the objects of the logical relation—are given. Here we are after special representations—what Descartes's calls "ideas"—of the purported objects. Let Madonna and Francesca be in fact one woman. This woman may conspire to confuse the population by creating the impression of two distinct persons. I may then seem to conceive of Madonna singing in a Hollywood club but firmly deny Francesca's involvement. Any projection on that basis of a numerical distinctness in reality would be mistaken.

This would not be so if the "ideas" in question were essentially representative of the worldly objects, so that distinct ideas would necessarily *reflect* distinct objects *of which* they were ideas. I am not aware of a place where Descartes provides us with such a theory of reflective ideas (though he says quite a lot—and offers interesting bits—about ideas in his Meditation III). Perhaps, in the end, his notion of a "complete idea" (alluded to in the quotation from the letter to Gibieuf) can be made to carry this load; that is, for distinct, complete ideas of mind and body, reflection would hold. Let us call such complete ideas C-ideas. In our present view, when we say, "It is conceivable that DM is not DB," we only seem to be speaking directly of the objects DM and DB. What we really are speaking of directly are the C-ideas. We thus really say, "In our conception, C (DM) ≠ C (DB)." But now, by the reflecting reality principle, we may infer that in reality DM is not DB.

I have at this point two things to say about this line of argument. First, even granting the foregoing, we would still have no result of *real* distinction. We would have the numerical distinction of DM and DB, very much consistent with the exclusion of any sense of "can" according to which the one can exist without the other. Second, the argument critically depends on developing Descartes's notion of complete idea, which I do in the next few pages. Then I return briefly to an evaluation of the present defense of a conceivability-based yet possibility-free proof of the numerical distinction of DM and DB.[7]

1.5. The Primacy of Whatness

The Third Way I: "Too Much" vs. "Too Little"

It is not quite clear to me where Descartes comes out in Arnauld's case. In his official reply (CSM II, 158), he cites three facts that mark a disanalogy between the geometric example and the mind-body situation:

(i) In the geometric example, neither the triangle nor the property P are "things" (substances), whereas both DM and DB are.
(ii) One may understand a right triangle T without property P but not think about P without thinking about right angles; but one can think—symmetrically, as it were—about mind without body and about body without mind.

---

7. See the notion of "conceptual fix" in 1.5 and the analysis of conceivability illusions in ch. 3, section 3.1.

(iii) One can understand T without thinking about P but not without any thought about the ratio between the hypotenuse and the two other sides; but one can think of the mind without reference to any kind of connection to a body.

Even if we grant the truth of (i)–(iii), I do not see how they address the core of Arnauld's objection, let alone provide a way out of it. At best, the points, especially (ii)–(iii), are the beginning of a general theory of what is involved in a complete idea of a given subject of conception. It is such a theory that will provide Descartes's response to Arnauld. I assume that Descartes's full answer to Arnauld must lie beyond these three short paragraphs.

What is it? Of the two responses discussed so far, Descartes is certainly not attracted by the primacy of possibility, Arnauld's own way out. It is rather the primacy of conceivability as a way out that is closer to Descartes's inclinations, in the fourth replies and in his letter to Gibieuf: De-modalize the real distinction argument; leave real possibility out of it; insist that DM and DB have been really conceived of apart; and thus, by means of the reflection principle, get the result that in reality DM is not DB.

Such a line of argumentation is not repulsive to Descartes. But the argument is, as it were, an argument in waiting: It still needs to supply a theory of conceptual fix on a subject. A theory of conceptual fix specifies what it takes a given thinker to *have* in his or her understanding as a particular target object, specifically, to manage to really conceive *that object* and not a mere aspect of it or some qualitatively similar twin object (the seeming of the object). We face here a quandary: Might not the constraints about what it takes to conceive some item x come from the very—conceivability-free—basic metaphysics of x?

Arnauld proposes one such metaphysical basis, the possibilities involving x. Let property F be modally impossible for x.

Suppose *F* has been conceived of some candidate item *y*. Then, Arnauld concludes, *y* is not *x*.

Arnauld may have been wrong about which metaphysical features—modal possibilities—do the constraining. But even if Descartes rejects Arnauld's way out, he must admit that some facts about *x* must constraint what it is to successfully conceive of *it*. Descartes must supply some such conceptual fix theory. As we shall see, he does.

So, we are looking for a third response to Arnauld's objection. Partly, we are looking here on behalf of Descartes. I cannot say that such a third response would be one literally enunciated by him in one specific, canonical paragraph. Indeed, I do not think there is any such single answer from Descartes but rather fragments of answers, pushing sometimes in one direction, sometimes in another. When we have the full third response, I hope it will turn out to be very much in tune with his general line of attack on the real distinction proof.

We are searching for a third way out in the hope of isolating Descartes's favorite response. But we are also searching because it is natural to imagine such a third way, given the first two responses. Both the first two ways out have virtues and vices. Using Descartes's own terminology, I will, instead of vices, speak of solutions that give us "too little" or "too much."

As I see it, Arnauld's response asserts too much in metaphysics and too little in epistemology:

(i) *Too much* in its possibility involvement: Too much is required for having a conceptual fix on a target *x*; that is, never run afoul of *x*'s necessary features.

(ii) *Too much* in the real distinction proof: If one were to defend a real distinction proof while adhering to Arnauld's theory of conceivability, one would *have* to ground the proof in a real possibility of disembodied existence for DM. Those interested in the dual key project—integrating DM and DB in a single man—would find such a real possibility to be too much, too strong a premise.

(iii) *Too little* in its epistemology: We have no reliable access to what we conceive. Arnauld's allowance for a gap between seeming and really conceiving is fine for some cases (the geometric example). But by claiming the gap across the board, we are left with too little about our manner of apprehension of mind and body; in this case, the concepts (ideas) through which we conceive the target objects are more reliable.

The second way out—the one stressing the primacy of conceivability—presents an opposite profile. It asserts too little in metaphysics and too much in epistemology:

(i) *Too little constraining of conceivability*. Having rejected Arnauld's possibility constraint, we swing to the other extreme—there is no constraint from the metaphysics of x on what it would take to have a conceptual fix on x.

(ii) *Too little in the real distinction proof*. We are provided with merely the numerical distinction of DM and DB and no blueprints for how DM can exist without DB.

(iii) *Too much in epistemology*. The approach asserts an across-the-board transparency thesis—seeming to conceive suffices for really conceiving. This may be too demanding for many ordinary empirical subjects of conception with nontransparent "essences"; it also seems incorrect for certain mathematical subjects like Arnauld's T.

The Third Way II: Two Ground Facts

It would be appealing to submit here a third way out, free of the preceding vices and sensitive to the virtues. Before we so proceed, let me add that such a proposal should respect what strikes me as two basic facts that have so far been neglected. Both facts seem to me intuitively right, prior to particular theories so far offered, and so basic that any theoretical reaction to Arnauld's case would want to respect them. The first basic fact—the *epistemic*—concerns the problem of what it takes to have a conceptual fix on an object x; the second—the *metaphysical*—concerns the whatness of x, what kind of object x is.

The epistemic fact is addressed to Arnauld. Consider his right triangle T. I believe both Arnauld and Descartes feel—at least at first blush—that we, and even practicing mathematicians, can successfully think of T and deny its necessary feature P. But we would not feel thus if the thinker did not respect in his conception features like triangle, many-sided body, figure with angles, and even figure with three sides and a right angle. So these features are more constitutive of having a mental hold on T than mere necessary accidents of T—for example, it satisfies property P, has in Riemann's geometry an angle sum that is not that of two right angles, has in Euclidean geometry an angle sum that is twice the atomic number of uranium minus four, and so on.

We find the same pattern when we think about empirical subjects. Consider Descartes's favorite, the river Loire. One may think of it and flout what may well be necessary of it: It originates in the Gerbier de Jonc Massif, it does not fall into the Indian Ocean and does not flow on the planet Mars, the liquid stuff flowing in it contains oxygen atoms, and so on. On the other hand, if one were to deny in one's conception that it is a river, one's claim to be thinking about the Loire would be endangered.[8]

This suggests that some among x's (necessary) features are constitutive to our conceptual fix. This much concerns an epistemological question about us. But it leads to one of metaphys-

---

8. I take it here as necessary about rivers (true in every way, such an item might have evolved while in existence) that, even as the item changes its course, it keeps originating in a given mountain range, does not fall into the sea at the other side of the globe, and carries in it give-and-take impurities H_2O molecules.

ics: Might not some among x's necessary features be "more" constitutive to what it is? Reconsider the triangle T. Surely it has infinitely many mathematical features—all of them necessary—that do not pertain to what it is.

What then is T? A right triangle; in turn, an extended body. The last two features articulate what this item is, the very *kind* of item it is. In contrast, many of its necessary features—I use here, with a twist, the medieval language of "necessary accidents"—do not concern what T is. Rather, they are subsequent to the kind-specifying predication. First we are given the subject: It is a right triangle. Only now, having articulated its whatness, we may ponder *how* this item might have been. We may find that throughout each and every way (mode) of its being, it could not have failed to satisfy property P; for that matter, it could not have failed to be Pythagoras' actually favorite figure (here the addition of "actually" makes this a *necessary* feature of T, given that it was indeed Pythagoras' favorite figure). The necessary accidents apply to an already fixed subject with antecedently given whatness—a right triangle.

In the same vein, let us consider another mathematical object, the number 4. Its being a number—and a positive integer—pertains to what it is. So does the feature of being the successor of 3. But 4 has many other necessary features: It solves the color map hypothesis in topology; it is twice the number of hydrogen atoms in a water molecule; it is the number of dimensions in a Minkowski space-time structure. These are all accidents 4 could not have failed to have. And yet they do not articulate what kind of subject 4 is.

The idea of what a given subject is, the kind of thing it is, is very primordial in Descartes's thinking. In various contexts, this—rather than any modal question about necessity—is his first question about the subject of investigation. He so asks about the triangle in Meditation V, as well as about mountains and about God; he so asks about the sun in Meditation III (in separating our different ideas about it from what that body is); and, of course, Meditation II is saturated with such questions about the piece of wax (on which much more later) and about the mind and the body, and it raises our primal question: What am I? In all, Descartes is after the kind of item involved, not just the listing of its accidents, necessary though they may be.

The theory about whatness-specifying features is part of the metaphysics of a given subject. But we see that it soon leads to epistemic corollaries. In the quest for natural constraints on what it takes to have a conceptual fix on a given object x, we look for metaphysically distinguished features of x. Arnauld proposes the necessary features. But they fail twice over. They fail epistemically because intuitively this demands too much. We all feel that arbitrary, hidden necessities about x cannot undo our mental hold on x. Arnauld's modal answer fails a second time in not distinguishing, now in the metaphysics of x, the *premodal* articulation of just what kind of thing this subject is from a subsequent business—how that subject (now already given) might have been, which ways it could have gone on to be.

I submit that both basic facts must be respected by a theory of complete ideas or conceivings about x. It now seems that a proper treatment of the epistemic basic fact might be a byproduct of respecting the metaphysical basic fact. In other words, a theory of genuinely thinking about x may rely on a theory of what x is. I believe that Descartes's remarks about complete ideas supply such a theory, and it is to this theory that I now turn.[9]

The Third Way III: Complete Ideas

Arnauld is uneasy about the lack of constraints in Descartes's theory of conceptual fix: "But someone might call this minor premiss into doubt and maintain that the conception you have

---

9. The preceding section introduces the distinction between what a thing is and how it is. I have discussed the distinction in a more general metaphysical, Descartes-free context in "The What and the How I," *Journal of Philosophy* (1991); and "The What and the How II," *Nous* (1996).

of yourself when you conceive of yourself as thinking, non extended, thing is an inadequate one..." (CSM II, 141). The letter to Gibieuf reports similar worries:

> You inquire into the principles by which I claim to know that the idea I have of something is not an idea made inadequate by the abstraction of my intellect... intellectual abstraction would consist in my turning my thought away from one part of the contents of the richer idea which I have in myself to another part with greater attention.... Of course, by abstraction we can obtain the idea of a mountain without a valley or of an upward slope without considering that the same slope can be traveled downhill. (PL, 123–124)

This, then, is the worry. It arises dramatically when the primacy of conceivability is assumed. This suggests that from the distinctness of the *ideas* associated with DM and DB, we conclude that in reality DM is distinct from DB. But what if DM and DB were one and the same—rather like Madonna and Francesca—and the two ideas arose here by intellectual abstraction?

The worry arises in the context of the primacy of conceivability solution, but its force is quite general. Descartes rejects Arnauld's theory of conceptual fix, that is, respect all necessities about x. Very well. But he seems to offer nothing instead. This opens the floodgates to wild claims of conceivability about x: No matter how off-base the conception of x, we still conceive of it. This cannot be Descartes's ultimate defense of the mechanism of conceivability.

It is not. Descartes tells us quite explicitly:

> There is a great difference between abstraction and exclusion. If I simply said that the idea which I have of my soul does not represent it to me as being dependent on a

body and identified with it, this would merely be an abstraction, from which I could only form a negative argument, which would be unsound. But I say that this idea represents it to me as a substance which can exist though everything belonging to body be excluded from it; from which I form a positive argument, and conclude it can exist without the body. (PL, 152[10])

The second text is the already quoted passage from a letter to Gibieuf:

The idea which I have of a thinking substance is complete in this sense and I have in my mind no other idea which is prior to it and joined to it in such a way that I cannot think of the two together while denying the one of the other. (PL, 124[11])

Here, in a couple of elegant paragraphs in later letters, Descartes encodes the essential ingredients of his "complete idea," a four-page answer to Arnauld in the fourth replies (CSM II, 156–160) and related remarks to Caterus in the first replies (CSM II, 85–86). What follows presents a way of understanding Descartes's notion of complete idea.

First, in the term "complete idea," the adjective characterizes a kind of *idea*. But Descartes also uses "complete" to modify "thing"; for example, in the reply to Arnauld, he keeps referring to the distinction between complete and incomplete things (and "entities"): "I took 'complete understanding of something' and 'understanding something to be a complete thing' as having one and the same meaning." And in the next paragraph, he says: "By a complete thing I simply mean a substance endowed

10. Letter to Mesland, May 2, 1644.
11. Letter to Gibieuf, January 19, 1642.

with the forms or attributes which enable me to recognize that it is a substance."

This is how I intend to understand the notion of completeness, that is, as relating primarily to things, to purported subjects. I will just read the complete understanding (idea) of something as an understanding (idea) of a complete thing.

Now, "complete" is a technical adjective. How are we to understand its intuitive import? When do we have on hand a complete thing? Arnauld offers one candidate: A story (a scenario, a conceiving) operates with a complete idea of x, that is, with an idea of the complete thing x iff the story (etc.) respects all of x's necessary traits. Descartes rejects this understanding as requiring "too much," and he seems to be right.

At the other extreme lies the worry of a story that is operating with a mere intellectual abstraction on x, a fixation on a mere "backside" of x. An example of such an incomplete (idea of an) entity is given in the letter to Gibieuf. Descartes mentions a discourse about a shape S without any reference to the substance *whose* shape it is. The example is repeated in the first replies (CSM, 86), and another one is added: To think of justice without thinking of the person who is just is to similarly introduce an incomplete entity.

Very well: On one end, we are dealing with mere aspects, modes, or abstractions from the full-blooded subject; at the other end, our conception of the subject is so full that it is overloaded with any necessary feature borne by the subject. We swing between too little and too much. Is there any natural balancing point here?

I should like it noted that the question posed is not about the *creation point* of a subject, as if we wondered how, by gluing enough properties together, we can conceive-into-being a real being. The question is rather about the limits of *subtraction* from a *given* real being, what Descartes describes as "exclusion" from a given subject. Alas, many readers, contemporaries of Descartes and contemporaries of us, think that the question is one of "philosophical (conceptual) creation": When have enough properties been thrown into the conceiver's pot to *create* a real subject? To which the answer should be: never. One never creates a subject—a real subject like Nixon or a fictional one like Hamlet—by gluing properties together. Rather the question is this: Of an already *given* subject x provided by the history of the world, what are the limits of subtractions from the list of its actual features, preserving all the while the sense that the story (conceiving) is still about x?[12]

The Third Way IV: Whatness vs. Necessity

Our question to Descartes is this: Suppose we are conceiving in the intended subtractive mode and suppose we are focused on a given subject x. What is the condition for success? Is there a natural balance point between requiring too much—do not tinker with the necessities about x—and requiring too little, whereby x itself is subtracted and lost?

I believe that Descartes submits that there is such a natural condition. It is the respect of what the thing is. To articulate what an item is is much less than providing its full list of necessary features [I assume, as did (WC) above, that its whatness is included in the necessary features list.] On the other hand, to preserve the whatness *of* the item is much more than to abstract *from* the item this or that aspect; in the latter, we merely focus on a perspective we happen to have on the item.

---

12. This much applies as well to fictional characters like Hamlet. Shakespeare did not generate Hamlet by gluing properties together. Rather, the world (here certain historical acts of the author, Shakespeare) provided Hamlet. We may now try to conceptually subtract some of Hamlet's features, for example, being melancholic. Of course, with fictional items we have to be careful about what Hamlet is in the story (a man and melancholic) and what he is outside the story (a fictional character). Various complications arise from this duality but they do not take away the main point: Real subjects—fictional or not—are not created by gluing properties together.

In assessing the answer I take Descartes to be giving, we must remind ourselves that we are dealing here with a *phenomenological* question: What captures best our sense that the story (conceiving) is still about the purported subject x? To this kind of question, we should not expect strict "algorithmic" rules. We test various candidates and find out—by trial and error—what kind of features get our intuitions satisfied. Descartes's answer, as I read it, is this: We may well subtract necessary features and still be speaking of the purported subject x. But subtract what-x-is, and gone with it is x itself. We are no longer subtracting *from* x; we are subtracting x. In Descartes's own language, we are no longer *excluding* from what x is its mere how; we are now *abstracting* from x a new item, a mere property or mode thereof.

The whatness condition seems right for empirical subjects; for example, consider Nixon. We may conceptually subtract from this man features philosophers have taken as necessary, for example, make him live 20 years earlier than he did or make him emerge from gametes other than those he actually emerged from; and though, of necessity, Nixon was the actual president of the United States in 1970, we may subtract this feature in the story. But if we subtract his being human, perhaps making him a frog or a crocodile, we are destroying the sense that the story is a coherent story about Nixon.

The condition seems pertinent for mathematical items. Consider Arnauld's triangle T. We may conceptually subtract the property P. Indeed, I believe that Pythagoras, thinking of T, may have conjectured to himself, "I bet P is not true of such right triangles," only to find to his surprise that T bears P after all. This often occurs in mathematical work: Mathematicians think about some (kind of) object x. On their way to eventually proving that x is F, they consider (and sometimes, convince themselves) that x is not F.

An interesting example is seen in a branch of mathematics called set theory. A certain story may be provided—about what sets are—that from a later perspective turns out to be (i) actually false about sets and (ii) as such, necessarily false. Nonetheless, the story is a coherent story about sets, preserving their very essence.

Here is a summary of such a story. The theory of sets is taken to describe a "real" universe of sets V_R. By one of set theory's own early results, V_R itself is not a set; it is a *plurality* of sets that is not itself collectible into one more set. When set theoreticians initially thought about the fundamental structural operations that generate the universe of sets, they articulated the following: We generate sets in *stages*. We start, in stage zero, by taking as our basis the empty set, the unique set without members. Given this basis, we go on to generate, at later stages, more sets. We have two such generative operations for the two kinds of stages we encounter. In any *successor* stage—the one after the first, the one after that, and so on—we take the power set, the set of all previously generated subsets, and make that power set the new universe. The second operation concerns *limit* stages of construction—the stage beyond the first, second, and so on—a stage we think of as the first infinite stage, dubbed the ω stage. At such a limit stage, we take the union of all previously available sets. Applying these operations on and on, we generate the universe of sets.

The question now is this: How many stages does it take to generate the full universe? Suppose we think that there are only ω many stages of generation. We get a universe with infinitely many sets, each of which is merely a finite set. In this universe of finite sets, no single set is itself infinite. We may call this *the universe of finite sets*, V_F. This story casts in modern set theoretic terms (as it were, with hindsight) what was probably the received view for generations of mathematicians who believed in the merely "potential infinite," a universe with infinitely many items but no single infinite item. This common view was questioned in the nineteenth century by the work of mathematicians like Bolzano, Dedekind, and Cantor.

Under the impulse of these nineteenth-century pioneers, it has become a received truth of modern set theory—by the first decade of the twentieth century—that on top of the sets of V_F, there are "larger" sets. Modern set theory asserts not only that the universe of hitherto generated finite sets is itself infinite but also that there exists at least one infinite *set*; for example, ω itself is such a set. Indeed, it goes on to assert that many such infinite sets exist. But the existence of at least one such set, set I, is sufficient for our purposes. I will assume it is true—in the real universe of sets V_R—that there is this set I. Since this is a mathematical truth, it is automatically a necessary truth.

We now confront the key question: Consider a story—the common view for centuries—that provides us with the universe of finite sets as the full domain of sets. By our hypothesis, this story is (i) not really true about sets and (ii) not really possible about them. Nonetheless, it is arguable that this is a coherent story about sets. The story does not respect *how many* sets there are, but it does respect *what* sets are. This last claim is defensible because the story—as articulated above—gives us the fundamental generative operations that produce sets. We omit some real sets from the story, but we don't omit what it is to be a set.[13]

---

13. (For the technically minded reader only): Of course, this example is presented here merely as an illustration. I do not mean to delve into the philosophy of set theory. What is more, many might think that the operations under which the universe of finite sets is closed do not exhaust what sets are. They may think so (i) because V_F is wrong about how many sets there are or (ii) because, although in principle a model may be wrong—it may omit some real sets—but still respect the essence of sets, the omitting of all infinite sets is incoherent. Why? Because it is constitutive of what sets are (of the "very idea" of set), that there is at least one infinite set.

I cannot address here the objections in detail. The second objection may seem to have much plausibility. I will only say that even if it were right, other examples of large infinite sets S—of fancier character—arise, in which all sides would agree that the existence of S is (i) true in the real universe, hence necessary, and yet (ii) not pertaining to the very essence of sets. For example, consider Ernst Zermelo, who stated early in the twentieth century the axiom that ω is a set, indeed, the least in size-infinite set. He did reveal

The moral so far is that we should not confuse consistency with possibility. With this in mind, let us go back to Arnauld's own original geometric example. It displays nicely the gap between consistency and possibility that I have been harping on. To prove property P of T, one needs the axiom of parallels of Euclidean geometry. Given that the axiom is true of Euclidean space, it is necessarily true, and so is T's bearing P. But we may consider models of the first four Euclidean axioms, which do not satisfy the axioms of parallels; that is, right triangles do not bear P. Nonetheless, it is arguable that beings living "inside" such a space and conceptualizing (visualizing) it non-Euclideanly may very well have the idea of a right triangle.

So it goes for the mathematical examples—a gap between real possibility and the weaker idea of consistency with what is x. In the present reconstruction, we read Descartes as looking for a similar gap between necessity and whatness in the mind-body real distinction proof. This leads to Descartes's third response to Arnauld.

Let us grant Arnauld that, of necessity, DM and DB coexist in a union inside the human being whose mind and body they are. I call this *the necessary union hypothesis*. We thus grant Arnauld the analogy he was seeking—just as triangle T is of

---

a way to number such infinite sets according to size, thus providing for the second infinite size, the third, and so on. But what about the ω place in this sequence, what is standardly referred to as $\aleph_\omega$? Is it also a set? Zermelo's own theory "forgot" to state principles that guarantee the existence of this set. The theory is consistent with there not being such a set. But given its actual existence in V_R, it is impossible that this set does not exist. Similar remarks apply to yet larger sets, for example, those called in set theory "the (strong) inaccessible" cardinals, whose theory was articulated by Zermelo later, in the 1930s. The objector who resists the present line of response will have to suggest that each such (existential) truth about sets is ipso facto pertaining to the essence of sets. I regard this as much too strong a claim. It does not distinguish arbitrary truths about sets from truths about what they are.

necessity bound to property *P*, subjects DM and DB are of necessity bound to each other.

Nonetheless, DM is distinct from DB. How so? What-DM-is is a *thinking thing*; what-DB-is is an *extended thing*. Thus DM is *by what it is (nature, essentially) thinking*. DB is not. Hence, by the distinctness of discernibles, DM and DB are two subjects. We may put this argument in a form analogous to that displayed by the possibility and conceivability arguments. That is, DM bears the property *consistent-with-what-it-is-to-not-be-extended*; DB does not bear this property. Thus DM and DB are numerically distinct. Also, the consistency-with-what-DM-is provides a coherent story, with unextended DM. It is not DB in the story. This last may be true because DB is in the story, but being essentially extended—hence, extended in this story, too—it is not DM. Stronger yet, DM may be distinct from DB in the story simply because there are no extended items in the story and thus, in particular, DB is not in it. As mentioned earlier, Descartes's Meditation II insists on the coherence of such a story. Assuming it, we have a sense according to which DM can exist apart from DB. We secure the real distinction: Even if it is not really possible, it is logically consistent with what DM is, being a thinking thing, that it exists (i) without any extended thing or (ii) without the specific extended thing, DB.

The Third Way V: Evaluation

All in all, Descartes's response follows the *structure* of Arnauld's own theory without accepting its overly strong premises. I thus see this third way out as having (i) logical, (ii) metaphysical, and (iii) epistemic advantages over the two other escape routes.

Logically speaking, we operate throughout with weaker premises (and sometimes they are not merely weaker; they seem truer). Whereas Arnauld projects real possibility from conceivability, Descartes merely projects a coherent story that might well represent no real possibility. Whereas Arnauld insists on real possibility of disembodied existence for a real distinction between DM and DB, Descartes requires merely separation in a coherent story (model). Whereas Arnauld demands respect for all of x's necessary features for a conceptual fix on x, Descartes requires merely respect for what x is.

Metaphysically speaking, the third way out allows for an element that might strike many modern thinkers about the mind-body problem as more likely than not—the necessary connection of the human mind and body. I, for one, would rather assume this at the outset and bar claims of the genuine possibility of the disembodied existence of DM. This is all the more poignant in the context of this book because of the second stage of our dual key project. In chapter 2, we are to integrate DM and DB as the mind and body of a single human being. Such an integrative theory assumes, at the very least, that the human mind and body—indeed this specific human mind and body of this specific human being—are necessarily connected.

Finally, this real distinction proof preserves an attractive epistemology of conceivability. Arnauld dispenses—across the board—with the sense that at least sometimes when we claim to have conceived of something, we are guaranteed to be reliable. He turns examples in which our access to the necessary properties of the subject is flawed into the paradigm for all cases of conceivability. This strikes me as oversweeping.

Arnauld may provide the right picture for subjects like the Loire, this table in front of me, the substance water, or the species tiger—subjects whose essence (what they are) involves scientific discoveries in chemistry, biology, and geology concerning the material composition of the external world. But the case of DM and DB seems categorically different, at least from Descartes's standpoint (which I am here trying to reconstruct).

Let someone assert that "what my mind is is a thinking being" and "what my body is is an extended thing." It is not clear what scientific discoveries—of the kind made about the nonfishood of whales and the noncompoundness of gold—may arise and give the lie to these assertions.

At one point in his critique of Descartes's method, Gassendi (in the fifth objections) says to Descartes:

> If we are asking about wine . . . it will hardly be enough for you to say "wine is a liquid thing, which is compressed from grapes, white or red, sweet, intoxicating" and so on. You will have to attempt to investigate and somehow its internal substance, showing how it can be manufactured from spirits, tartar, the distillate and other ingredients in such and such quantities and proportions. Similarly . . . you must see that it is certainly not enough for you to announce that you are a thing that thinks and doubts and understands etc. You should carefully scrutinize yourself and conduct a kind of chemical investigation of yourself, if you are to succeed in uncovering and explaining to us your internal substance. (CSM II, 193)

To this Descartes replies:

> You want us, you say "to conduct a kind of chemical investigation" of the mind, as we would of wine. This is indeed worthy of you, O Flesh, and of all those who have only a very confused conception of everything and so do not know the proper questions to ask about each thing. (CSM II, 248–249)

The rudeness is gratuitous, but Descartes's point is well taken. Scientific investigation may reveal to us that what wine is is not what we took it to be; and though we thought we were conceiving something about what seemed to be wine, the subject of the conceiving was not really wine. Thus we were not really conceiving—whatever it was—of *wine*. This is not true of our mind and body. Science may divulge to us various truths about both mind and body, perhaps necessary truths. But our basic conception of what each one of us is is not threatened by future chemical discoveries. If we seem to conceive of mind and body—of a thinking and an extended thing—we are really doing what we seem to be doing. And so our two conceivability-based results have a bite:

(C1) We seem to conceive of DM as distinct from DB; thus, we really conceive the numerical distinction.

(C2) We seem to conceive of DM as existing without DB; thus we really conceive the real distinction.

We see how the metaphysics and the epistemology fall into their natural places. Metaphysically, we prove, from conceivability-free facts about whatness, that

(W1) What DM is is not what DB is; thus, DM is distinct from DB.

Also, we prove that

(W2) It is consistent with what DM is that it exists and DB does not; thus, DM and DB are really distinct.

So much is metaphysics. But we have a reliable epistemology with which to come to know it. Our access—conceptual fix—on what DM is and what DB is is not as tenuous as Arnauld's pessimism would have it. In this domain—if not when we think about whales, gold, and triangles—our complete ideas are reflective of the whatness of the items they are ideas of. By means of (C1) and (C2), we have reliable access to (W1) and (W2).

Thus, we conclude chapter 1—focused exclusively on the duo of DM and DB—in a rather optimistic vein. It remains to be seen whether the optimism can be sustained when we bring in Descartes's third player, the full-blooded human being; whether our whatness assignments, to DM and DB, can then still be the purely generic "a thinking thing" and "an extended thing"; whether, in turn, we would still be able to claim that it is consistent with what DM is that it exists without DB; and finally, whether it would then still be really conceivable of DM that it exists without DB.

1.6. Appendix: Conceivability— Does Epistemology Precede Metaphysics?

Descartes, Arnauld, and Kripke

Three arguments for the discernibility of DM and DB were mentioned—from conceivability, possibility, and whatness. We experimented with grounding the discernibility in both the possibility and whatness properties. But we never quite allowed ourselves to consider the conceivability argument in and of itself. What could be said in defense of such an *autonomy of conceivability* thesis?

As we saw, Arnauld took an unbending negative stand on this—there can be no "autonomous" conceivability argument; what is *really* conceivable is dependent on what is *really* possible. In our own third-way argument, we softened this by making real conceivability free of arbitrary possibility facts. Nonetheless, it did turn out to depend on real whatness facts. Thus, in both Arnauld's discussion and ours, the metaphysical precedes the epistemological.

The question before us is whether we cannot do any better on behalf of "the autonomy of conceivability" conception; if we cannot, we need to know why; that is, is there something with the force of a *result* that blocks us here?

In what follows, I would like to consider what may well be the most powerful attempt to date to explore the question, one arising from Saul Kripke's *Naming and Necessity*. Although I have vowed not to bring into this book modern analyses that go beyond the context of Descartes and Arnauld, Kripke's discussion does take us beyond this period. But I believe that this one reference beyond the seventeenth century provides genuine illumination over the very issues discussed by Descartes and Arnauld. My hunch is that, learning of Kripke's analysis, Descartes and Arnauld would have immediately seen the pertinence of his remarks to the "autonomy of conceivability" thesis they were arguing over.

Kripke presents a beguiling intermediate position between Arnauld and Descartes. In many ways, he is very close to Arnauld because of Kripke's fundamental distinction between seeming to conceive and really conceiving. Also, like Arnauld, Kripke emphasizes that in the most general case, empirical or mathematical, we may turn out to be wrong about what we really conceive of; it all depends on whether we respected the essence of the target object, and this essence may not be transparent to us. In Kripke, as in Arnauld, the epistemological is reined in by the metaphysical.

At the same time, Kripke sides with Descartes, against Gassendi and Arnauld, in conceivings of *mental* items. Like Descartes, Kripke takes conceivings of items such as wine in one way, conceivings of mental items in quite a different way. Like Descartes, Kripke hopes to avert, in this realm, the gap between seeming to conceive and really conceiving. It is my conviction that because of this nuanced intermediate position, Kripke's analysis generates a "best possible" result for the autonomy of the conceivability thesis. Indeed, so nunanced is the result that it does not uniformly treat all things mental. The result has its surprises.

Logic Matters: De Re vs. De Dicto Arguments

Explorers of a conceivability argument—like Descartes and Kripke—hope to achieve two aims: (i) a *metaphysically* simple discernibility argument, by means of the genuine property *conceivably-exists-without-the pertinent-physicalium*, and (ii) an *epistemologically* transparent argument, affordable by the direct accessibility of the conceivability data. In the process of moving back and forth between the metaphysics and the epistemology, we run the danger of mixing the logical forms of different arguments. To avert the danger, we need to separate two types of arguments from conceivability. I will first draw the distinction in Kripke's framework, where these logical differences are explicitly available, and then extend it to Descartes's conceivability argument.

The mind-body arguments of Saul Kripke in his *Naming and Necessity* illustrate the two types of argument I have in mind. Kripke is not directly focused on the distinction of mind and body (though he does speak of his arguments from time to time as showing the distinctness of, e.g., the man Descartes and that man's body). In the main, Kripke attends to the distinction between the mental state (phenomenon) of pain and the brain state (phenomenon) of the firing of C fibers (henceforth, FCF). Also, his focus is on imaginability rather than conceivability. But the distinction we are after applies across these variations; as mentioned, it is a distinction of logic. It is between what I call *the de re argument* and *the de dicto argument*.

In Kripke's de re possibility argument, we may use whatever expression we wish to pick out certain purported objects—say, a certain pain I had at 6 A.M. and a certain related brain state occurring in my brain at 6 A.M. We may, for example, pick the two purported items by speaking of my least favorite sensation on Monday morning and the last event recorded on the MRI (magnetic resonant imaging) machine at 6 A.M. Let us use A for whatever such term we use to pick the pain, B for whatever term we use to specify the brain state.

Kripke's de re argument calls on the following single, nonlogical premise:

(Ko) A could have existed without B.

Thus, (Ko) is read to have the following structure: A certain object A—bears a certain modal property—*could have existed without* B. Surely B does not have this modal property. And so, by the distinctness of discernibles, Kripke may conclude that A is numerically distinct from B. Thus, the sensation is not the brain event. We may, of course, wonder about the truth of the key premise. But it is clear that the argument is free of any speculation about our (linguistic) representations of mind and body.

In contrast, Kripke's de dicto argument essentially involves theories about *language*. Kripke considers the terms "pain" and "FCF." He asserts about both that they pick out in every counterfactual possibility the same state (phenomenon) that they actually pick out. In this, they are different from such designators as "my least favorite sensation" and "the state recorded last on the MRI of my brain." These designators may each pick different phenomena in different possibilities. The phenomena of pain and FCF are what, respectively, these two designators actually pick out. But there is a possibility in which "my least favorite sensation" picks out the sensation of headache, and "the last event recorded on my MRI" refers to the firing of H fibers. In that possibility, the headache sensation is my least favorite sensation and the firing of H fibers is the last state to be recorded on my MRI. Kripke calls *rigid* those designators that keep picking up through all the possibilities what they actually pick up. He now asserts the first premise of his de dicto argument:

(K1) "Pain" and "FCF" are rigid designators.

Next, Kripke takes the English sentence "Pain is the firing of C fibers" to express the identity "Pain = FCF." We encounter here another linguistic assumption: The form of the English sentence is that of an *identity*. I doubt the assumption but act in what follows merely as an expounder of Kripke's argument. We are now ready for Kripke's second de dicto premise:

(K2) "It is possible that pain ≠ FCF" expresses a truth.

This is the analog of his direct de re modal property intuition, (K0). But it is merely an *analog*. With (K0), we had the straight predicative claim: This subject, pain, could have existed without that brain state *B*. The modal locution "possibly" (or "could") applies to "exists without *B*" to form a complex modal predicate. This predicate is said to hold of the phenomenon of pain. In the de dicto argument, the modal locution "It is possible that" acts as a sentential modifier, applying not to a genuine property but to a sentential representation—the whole claim (in latin, *dictum*), "Pain ≠ FCF." This sentence is said to be possibly true. Together, (K1) and (K2) deliver

(K3) "Pain ≠ FCF" is true (in reality).

It is quite clear that the de dicto argument rests critically on various semantic doctrines about the representations used in our dicta. One such assumption, (K1), concerns the terms "pain" and "FCF." For example, if these two representations meant something like "Almog's least favorite sensation" and "the event last recorded on the Almog MRI," (K1) would be false. The de dicto argument would have failed, even if the de re argument remained unaffected.

Many philosophers of language before Kripke did believe something like this about the meaning of the terms "pain" and "FCF." Some continue to hold on to such a semantic theory even after Kripke. I mention this not as a skeptic about Kripke's theory of language. Quite the contrary: I simply want us to take notice of the fact that the de dicto argument depends on extra assumptions about the nature of our linguistic representations.

The distinction between the two types of arguments extends in a natural way to the conceivability case. The de re conceivability argument assumes this one premise:

(C0) Pain is conceivable-without-FCF.

As before, (C0) is really two-tiered, but both tiers are metaphysical- and language-free. The first tier is that *conceivably so and so* is indeed a genuine property of things, borne independently of how the thing is specified. The second is that *conceivable-without-FCF* is borne by pain. Assume both: Then, surely, FCF does not bear the property. Thus, pain is not FCF.

Like its modal twin, the de dicto conceivability argument is more complex. We need first an assumption about our representations of pain and the related brain state, assumptions about what Descartes calls "our ideas" of pain and brain states. We may want to distinguish here, too, between representations like "pain" and "my least favorite sensation" and, respectively, between "the firing of C fibers" and "the state last recorded on my MRI."

One basis for differentiating is this: When I employ the representation "my least favorite sensation" in conceivings (Descartes would say, "in my understanding"), my mind has the freedom to alter what the representation *actually* stands for. It actually stands for the sensation of pain, but I can employ it in my understanding to get to the sensation of tasting fish. I can alter what is being picked out while sticking to the conventional meanings of the words used; for example, "sensation" still means sensation, in my conceiving exercise. In contrast, the word "pain" is resistant to any such conceivability-induced alteration. When I deploy it, thinking to myself, "Let me conceive that pain . . . " I may have some freedom about which predicates I apply to pain in the story constructed; but it is to *pain*—the old real sensation—that I apply these predicates.

We may summarize this difference by calling representations like "pain" and "the firing of C fibers" *reality-bound*: Even in conceiving exercises, they are employed to pick out the very items they pick out ordinarily, outside of conceiving exercises. Representations such as "my least favorite sensation" and "the last state recorded on my MRI" are not reality-bound. I shall call them *unbound*—my conceivings are free to endow them with new referents.

We are now ready to state the first assumption of the de dicto conceivability argument:

(C1) "Pain" and "FCF" are reality-bound designators.

We next need the assumption that

(C2) "It is conceivable that pain ≠ FCF" expresses a truth.

With both (C1) and (C2) given to us, we may conclude that

(C3) "Pain ≠ FCF" is true (in reality).

Has Transparent Epistemology Triumphed?

We have distinguished the de re argument from the de dicto variant. A natural question arises in both the possibility and conceivability cases: Why would one rely on the much more complex de dicto argument? After all, given the truth of its discerning premise, the de re discernibility is logically simpler. It is also much closer to the intuitive way in which we often seek a separation of two tightly connected candidates—we work through and through at the level of objects and properties, language notwithstanding, to find a discerning property. So, there remains the mystery: Why wheel in the much more complex de dicto argument?

The key lies in my passing remark, "given the truth of its discerning premise." The question is this: What on earth would "give" us this truth? On what basis may we assert the first premise of the de re argument? We seem in urgent need of an epistemological basis for our argument, of premises that are not only *true* but also *known* for certain (known a priori, known by sheer reflection, etc.).

This is where the de dicto argument becomes appealing. The hope is that by not operating directly on objects and properties but on our representations, it provides media known to us in a special way. Granted, the argument would get us to the bottom line only in a roundabout way. But, in the end, the price of the complexity seems negligible compared with the gain of a transparent epistemological basis. I believe it is this kind of reasoning that leads Descartes, and three centuries later, Kripke—both illustrious de re metaphysicians—to fall back on the de dicto argument.

Let us trace the epistemological gains promised by the de dicto argument. Consider Kripke's main de dicto premise, (K1)—"It is possible that pain ≠ FCF"—is true. De-representation rather than de-object as the claim is, in itself it still provides no special epistemic basis for assessment. We may well wonder why "taking" the sentence "Pain ≠ FCF" to another "possible world" and evaluating it for truth "over there" is any more epistemically transparent than asking directly, here in actuality, whether this phenomenon, pain, bears the modal property *possibly exists without FCF*? In both cases, it seems that we are involved with a primitive modal "fact," that thus and such is possible.

The de dicto arguer may retort that we think our access to evaluations of sentences ("dicta") in possible worlds is markedly more intimate than to modal properties of objects here in actuality. A reason to think so is provided by Kripke's bringing into de dicto evaluations the faculty of the *imagination*. In speaking of the evaluation of sentential representations in possible worlds, he speaks of trying (succeeding or failing) to imagine a situation in which the sentence is true or false. If a representation "*a* is *F*" is imaginable-by-the-mind, Kripke is happy to pronounce it possible for *a* to be *F*; if not, not.

We seem en route to justifying the dream ticket. We have on hand a logically sound argument (by means of possibility evaluations in "worlds" and the reflection of this onto actuality by rigid designators) sustained by a sound epistemology—the imagination providing the access to these evaluation worlds. In all, this is a swift victory over a tricky dilemma.

Seeming to Imagine vs. Really Imagining

The foregoing may be a favorite of many modern metaphysicians; it may even seem to be Kripke's own account, but it is not his *real* account. Kripke's notion of possibility (necessity) is based on many a posteriori (empirical), actual facts. For example, it is because water is actually made of oxygen that it is necessarily so; because gold actually has atomic number 79, it is necessarily so; because Madonna and Francesca are actually one and the same woman, they necessarily make one woman only. In all such cases, the delimitation of possibilities succeeds the facts of actuality. On the other hand, it surely *seems* to be easy to imagine, as Kripke himself admits, that water exists without oxygen, that gold is a compound, and that Madonna and Francesca make two distinct women. If imaginability were to be our guide, Kripke's notion of "metaphysical" possibility would be all but lost.

And so, in spite of the initial seeming priority of imaginability over possibility, Kripke's real account runs the other way around—water is not *really* imaginable without oxygen *because* it is not possible for water to exist without oxygen. Real imaginability about an object x is dependent on and posterior to what is really possible for x. Thus, real imaginability has now become as epistemically nontransparent as real possibility. The victory over our dilemma was too swift.

Kripke contrasts real imaginability with another notion, *seeming* imaginability. Seeming imaginability is meant to be closer to our first-impression intrinsic judgments, prior to subsequent empirical information about identity, biological origin, and chemical structure. With seeming imaginability we may regain a transparent epistemology, but at a price: A gap has now opened between what is seemingly imaginable about an item x and what is really imaginable about it. In sum: Whereas real imaginability is determined by real possibility, seeming imaginability determines merely seeming possibilities.

Kripke never quite offers a canonical theory of *what* it is we relate to when we seem to imagine this table (water, gold, etc.). At least two informal suggestions are made. The first is that to seemingly imagine x, say, water, is to really imagine *the seeming of water*, to relate to the sensation (look, feel, etc.), the phenomenological presentation, associated with water. This would make the object of seeming imagination shift from the external, real-world item—the wooden table or H$_2$O—to an internal, phenomenological quality, the how-it-seems.[14]

A second suggestion, also developed with great force by Kripke, runs like this: When we say that we seem to imagine water without oxygen, we mean that we have really imagined another substance that is qualitatively indiscernible from real water. Thus, he who says, that for example, he seems to imagine that this wooden table is made of ice is really asserting that another object, looking like this table, is really imaginable (and indeed is really possibly) made of ice.

In either explanation of seemings, we now confront a dilemma. To get a logically sound argument, one concerning the target object x (Madonna, the table, water, etc.), we can rely only on real imaginability (and, in turn, real possibility). However, we have no irrefragable access to real imaginability facts. On the other hand, we do know by sheer introspection what we seem to imagine. But, alas, seeming-imagination facts do not concern the pertinent target objects; involved are either mere seemings or worldly objects that are distinct, even if qualitatively indiscernible, from the target objects. And so, in our search for a discernibility argument for object x (say, from y), we run the risk of pronouncing a successful discerning on the basis of mistakenly identifying x with an indiscernible qualitative twin $t(x)$. Meanwhile, in reality, things run exactly the opposite way—x is necessarily identical with y; it is the qualitative twin $t(x)$ that is necessarily distinct from x $(=y)$. Kripke's admonition is that when it comes to real possibility-imaginability, nothing is quite what it seems.

---

14. See Saul Kripke, *Naming and Necessity* (Cambridge, Mass.: Harvard University Press, 1980), pp. 144–152.

Is Nothing Quite What it Seems?

If Kripke's bottom line were literally that nothing whatsoever is quite what it seems, he would have ended up where Arnauld's objection left us. But Kripke's principle is a touch more restricted—nothing *external* is quite what it seems. This leaves us with a realm where at least some things are what they seem. One such item, submits Kripke, is the phenomenon of pain.

The nature ("essence") of real pain is its seeming, the how-it-feels. Alternatively, something qualitatively indiscernible from pain is, for Kripke, pain all over again. Essential to being this kind of thing, pain, is the having of the qualitative characteristic.

Assume this much and then consider the hypothesis that I have merely seemingly imagined pain. If so, I have imagined the seeming of pain or really imagined something qualitatively indiscernible from pain. But then I have really imagined pain.

In this special case, and perhaps with other essentially qualitative items, we may successfully base our de dicto possibility on transparent imaginings after all. We seem to imagine "Pain ≠ FCF"; thus, we really imagine "Pain ≠ FCF"; and thus "Pain ≠ FCF" is possibly true—hence, actually true.[15]

---

15. I have presented Kripke's argument in a stronger way than he intends. His apparatus was made to "positively" assert that it is possible that pain is distinct from FCF and, thus assert that it is actually distinct from it. Taken more *de jure*, Kripke merely makes in his work the following negative point: The exposure of certain scenarios (e.g., that water is distinct from H_2O) as mere seeming possibilities does not extend to the case of "Pain is distinct from FCF." I have taken the extra step here of making Kripke assert that given the failure to expose an illusion, the seeming possibility is a real possibility.

I should point out that I stick to the role of an expounder of Kripke's views on pain. I take Kripke to be proposing that its phenomenological quality exhausts its list of necessary features. For myself, I have doubts about this on Kripkean grounds. It is Kripke who inspires us, in *Naming and Necessity*, to depart from Hume's famous doctrine that there are no necessary connections between distinct existences. To the contrary, everything real is necessarily connected to, or dependent on, other real things. Notable

Three Morals from Kripke's Result

I draw three morals from this discussion of Kripke. The first concerns the general question of relying on the imagination in discernibility arguments; the second, the special case of pain; the third, any extension to Descartes's mind.

1. *Imaginability*. In the general case of a discernibility argument over an arbitrary object x, the accessible mechanism of imaginability offers no solace. We cannot rule out a gap between seeming to imagine x and really imagining x. What is more, the question of whether, in some special cases, we are gap-immune depends on prior facts about the *nature* (whatness, essence) of x: If all there is to what x is is how it seems, we are gap-immune; if not, not.

And so, in the general case, we cannot do better than our initial de re discernibility (possibility, conceivability) arguments, with their "x is F" e.g. *x is possibly (conceivably) G*, subject-predicate structure. Either we have (i) the real subject x but with no transparency of its bearing of the predicate F, or

---

among such connections is the fundamentality of its dependence on its *generators*, the items and processes without which the real item in question would not have come into history. I take pain—and other mental phenomena—to be as real as physical constituents of the world. And thus, I don't see my pain at 6 A.M. as just mysteriously "jumping into existence." If, as a matter of causal fact, it was the firing of FCF in my brain that generated my pain, if indeed every pain event turns out to be generated by an FCF firing, then I would be very inclined to argue that there is no real possibility of pain unless FCF brings it about. The phenomenological quality of pain would still be distinct from the FCF that brings it about, and the two would be of different natures (essence). But once an FCF event occurred, of necessity pain would be felt. I have discussed the dependence of all reals on other reals in my own work; see, for instance, "The What and the How I, II," op. cit. Among others in the contemporary literature who have expressed similar criticisms of Kripke's views (while acknowledging some of his critical intuitions) are Tom Nagel, "Conceiving the Impossible and the Mind Body Problem," *Philosophy* (1999) and Torin Alter, "Essence, Necessity and the Mind Body Problem," manuscript, University of Alabama, 1999. In my discussion of Kripke here, I bracket away my own views about pain.

else we have (ii) the transparency of the applicability of the predicate F but not to the real subject x.

2. *Pain*. What closes the gap for seeming imagination in the special case of pain? Kripke turns to prior intuitions about essence (whatness, nature): With pain, though not, say, with water, the seeming of the phenomenon is what the (essence of the) very phenomenon is. This assertion about the essence (whatness, nature) of pain and water is not, in turn, dependent on what is imaginable. Our explanation has reached rock bottom. Our success in imagining x proper is explained in terms of what x is, not the other way round.

3. *Extension to Mind*. Is Kripke's principle for this one kind of mental phenomenon, pain, extendable in general to the mental, for example, to discernibility arguments about the mind in general?

Two remarks are in order at this point. First and to reiterate, even if Kripke's pain strategy were extendable to the mental in general, it would only emphasize the priority of whatness facts over imagination facts. We would have to argue that our seeming to imagine Descartes's mind, or a certain thinking thing x, is really imagining x. Here, as elsewhere, it is the essence of the mind that would determine whether it has really been imagined (conceived).

This brings us to the second remark. Our question is this: Kripke emphasizes in the case of pain the essentiality of the purely internal qualitative character. The principle may extend to other mental experiences. Is it extendable to everything mental?

We must separate two kinds of items in the allusion to "everything mental." On the one hand, we may be concerned with *subjects*, what Descartes refers to as "substances." So DM is such a subject, and the man René Descartes is another such subject (whether, for Descartes, it is indeed a substance will be discussed in chapter 2). On the other hand, we may be concerned with mental *predicates*, for example, "is thinking about water," "is thinking that water is wet," and "is intending to get some water." I take it that Kripke's discussion of pain was focused on the kind of predicate it is, that is, what is involved in applying "is in pain" or "feels pain" to some subject, say, the man Jones.[16]

The extension of Kripke's pain strategy to mentality-involving subjects—be it the mind DM or the man Descartes—invites major questions that have to do with according these items the status of "substances." Chapters 2 and 3 are dedicated to this issue, and it is within this context that imaginability of such subjects will be discussed (see, for instance, the sections on conceivable separability and conceivability illusions in chapter 3). But even before a thorough analysis, it is quite clear that the extension of the pain thesis to such subjects is very problematic. One way to realize the problem is this: Surely, if Kripke's thesis is not extendable to mental predicates such as "thinking about water" and "thinking that water is wet," it will not extend to the mental subjects who entertain such thoughts. If the mental states of such subjects are not exhausted by their phenomenological character, it may be argued that the subjects that bear those states do not have their identity so exhausted. (I do not argue this point here). And so, I will concentrate here on the most likely extension of Kripke's thesis—from experiential predicates to mental predicates in general.[17]

---

16. Kripke's discussion is rather informal on this matter. It is surely possible to read his remarks as applying to some sort of (higher order) subject, a certain *species* of mental states, in the way we can view, for example, tiger as a species of biological organisms. I, for one, (in "The What and the How" and "Nothing, Something, Infinity") so view tiger, water, and other worldly kinds, and I would so view pain, thirst, and so on. But the context of Kripke's discussion makes it quite likely that his remarks on "states" (of pain) are directed at a theory of mental properties such as "is in pain." The problems I mention below about extending Kripke's view to the mental in general do not depend on whether we read him, with regard to pain, as predicate- or subject-oriented.

17. As mentioned, (illusions of) conceivability of *subjects* like DM and the man Descartes will occupy us in chapter 3.

From Descartes's perspective, Kripke's focus (i) on sensations, as opposed to thinkings, and (ii) on the mechanism of imagination, as opposed to conceiving, is doubly ironic. Descartes took both Kripke's mental targets and the scanning technology as exactly those that are *not* distinctive of the mind proper. Rather, they show essential dependence on the body (and the brain in particular) and its *perceptual* powers. But let us not give up on the extension of Kripke's strategy just because Descartes saw a great gulf between perceptual (imaginative) states and purely intellectual states. Let us ask in a neutral vein whether the extension from "is in pain" to, say, "is thinking that water is wet" is feasible.

Consider, then, taking experiences, intentional action states, and thinking states (to cite three categories of mental states) as fundamental to a human mind. The critical point here is that right away it is far from obvious that intentional action and thinking states are exhausted by their purely qualitative, "phenomenological" character. Contemporary philosophy has stressed quite the opposite about such cognitive states. Standard examples in the philosophy of mind allude to two agents, Castor and Pollux, that are in the same phenomenological state—for example, enjoy in their heads the same "seeming of water"—but who nonetheless entertain two different thoughts. It is concluded that the two are in different thinking (types of) states. This is so simply because Castor interacted, solely on this planet, throughout his life with liquid H_2O whereas Pollux, confined to some other planet, interacted only with the qualitatively similar but chemically distinct liquid XYZ. In a similar vein, Castor may form the intention to drink some water but Pollux may form quite a different intention. This much seems true in spite of their common, inner qualitative feel (say, the feel of thirst).[18]

---

18. (N.B.: This footnote involves "technical" matters in "advanced" philosophy of language.) The intuitions I mention have been emphasized by Tyler Burge in many writings—see, for example, "Other Bodies," in

The preceding intuitions about the identity of thoughts (intentions) and thinking states have been supported by various arguments. Those who would like to extend Kripke's pain-strategy will have to refute the arguments. On the other hand, if we accept them, as I am inclined to, the extension of Kripke's thesis is blocked.

Suppose that two agents—myself, here on earth, and some twin, Max, on the other planet—engage, respectively, in imaginings of Castor and Pollux. I imagine Castor thinking that water is wet. Max imagines, as he would put it in his dialect, that Pollux is thinking that water is wet. Asked to enlarge on our experiences, both of us may describe an agent, in the pose of a thinker, and in his head visions of a transparent liquid,

---

Thought and Object, ed. A. Woodfield (London: Blackburn, 1982). In my own view, an even more radical thesis about cognition is defensible in which many thought (and other cognitive) states are essentially *relational*, relating agent and worldly item. This is not to be confused with another Burge claim (e.g., in his "De re Belief," *Journal of Philosophy* 1977) that many thoughts are essentially de re. Burge uses "de re" for what are really some special de dicto thoughts, thoughts involving quasi-demonstrative *representations*. As I read it, Burge's work is part of the classical project of reducing what I call relational thoughts to de dicto thoughts, although those that involve quasi-demonstrative representations. A *locus classicus* of this project is David Kaplan's "Quantifying In," *Synthese*, 1968. Burge's point is to amend Kaplan's initial reduction by giving, in the de dicto language, representations that are not purely qualitative but quasi demonstrative. In contrast, here I mean by "relational" or "essentially de re" thoughts essentially of the very object—thoughts with a direct, representation-free relation, binding the thinker Castor and his thought object, this table, the substance water, and so on. This view denies any reduction to a de dicto form in which the agent relates to a dictum (thought, proposition). The view I support may seem natural when we report acts of reference to and visual perceptions of the table, as reported, for example, by "Castor sees (refers to) the table." I extend it to our reports of thoughts of (beliefs about) the table. I have written, in a technical vein, on such matters in "The Subject Verb Object Class I, II," in *Philosophical Perspectives*, 1998 and "The Language to Describe Our Cognitive Lives" (to appear). Here I do not rely on my own stronger theses. The point in the text rests on Burge's now familiar view about the individuation of de dicto thoughts.

pouring down from the sky, and so on. The phenomenological description would be very much the same. We seem to imagine the same of Castor and Pollux. Do we really imagine the same? I imagine Castor thinking one thought—that H_2O is wet. Max is imagining Pollux thinking a distinct thought—that XYZ is wet.

The gap between seeming to imagine and really imagining has reopened because the nature of the objects—here the thoughts entertained by Castor and Pollux—is not exhausted by their phenomenological character. When what we conceive (imagine) is not purely phenomenological, seeming to imagine a target is not guaranteed to be a real imagining of it.

In more general terms, the following moral emerges: What has turned out to be the fundamental fact is not some imagination exercise but a whatness fact, that is, the nature of thinking states, as opposed to pain states. And so, I conclude the appendix very much in the way I concluded the text before the appendix. What we need primarily is not so much a dissection of the workings of imaginability and conceivability. What we need is more reflection on the nature of the objects about which we have these imaginings (conceivings). We need more insight into the nature of the three essential Cartesian factors—the human mind, the human body, and the human being. This is the task of chapter 2.[19]

---

19. I have not taken final leave of the question of conceivability. I go back to it in some detail, after the nature of the human mind, body, and being has been analyzed. See, for instance, chapter 3.

TWO

Integrative Dualism

2.1. The Prove Too Much/Prove Too Little Dilemma

In chapter 1 I argued for the real distinctness of the human mind and body, specifically Descartes's DM and DB, under four assumptions:

(i) *Complete subjecthood*. DM and DB are complete subjects.
(ii) *Modal inseparability*. DM and DB necessarily coexist.
(iii) *Conceivable existential separability*. It is conceivable of DM (describable in a scenario consistent with what DM is) that it exists without DB.
(iv) *Whatness separability*. DM and DB make different kinds of things.

However, as really distinct as DM and DB may be, we are only halfway through. As I have emphasized from the beginning of this book, the point of the two-stage Cartesian conception of man is this: The real distinction of the human mind and body is to be established so that it can next be embedded in a genuine subject—the real man, the human being *whose* mind and body they make.

As I read Descartes, it is only upon the completion of the full two-stage project that he would feel he had succeeded. But, alas, here precisely lies our predicament—the separate demands of the two stages pit them against each other. We seem to be prisoners of a dilemma I have called, following Descartes's own terminology in his reply to Arnauld, *the prove too much/prove too little dilemma.*

Let us recall the way in which the dilemma is generated. If we make the separability of DM and DB strong enough to count as a real distinction, we prove "too much." We assert a real possibility of disembodied existence for DM and thus a strong sense of self-sufficiency. When we now put this one self-sufficient being together with another such self-sufficient being, the body, we no longer get a real natural unity—a full-blooded human subject—but a "late-in-the-day" unity of composition, a derivative compound. This is the horn of proving too much.

To amend things, we might start by carefully protecting the primality of the full human being. But whatever subsequent separation by conceivability experiments we accord to the mind and body, it is not enough to establish them as distinct complete subjects that can exist without the other. This is the horn of proving too little.

A dilemma and, in its wake, a worry—in developing Descartes's conception of the real man, something in our quartet of assumptions from chapter 1 has got to give. Of course, it will not be the assumption of modal inseparability. But the three other assumptions seem vulnerable.

First, whatness separability is in some danger: Will we still stick with the rather generic essence assignment—merely "thinking" and "extended"—to the human mind and body? Might we not have to mention that what they are is intrinsically the mind and body *of* a human being? In like manner, might we not have to give up—as against (iii)—*any* existential separability between mind and body? Of course, we have already denied—with modal inseparability—that there is any real possibility of DM existing without DB. But now that we contemplate articulating what each is in terms of the human being whose mind and body they are, will we not have to deny even the weaker sense of conceivable existential discernibility? Finally, the darkest worry of them all: As we are bent on stressing the primality of the real man René Descartes (RD), will we not end up with (i) refuted? Descartes's mind and body will turn out to be mere *modes* of this man. Gone will be the claim of DM and DB to be two complete subjects.

2.2. Separatist Dualism: Four Basic Annotations

A dilemma and, in its wake, many worries—none of this gets off the ground in the most popular reading of Descartes, *separatist dualism*. This classical dualism contrasts with the two-stage picture that appears below under the title "Integrative Dualism." It is time to lay out the main tenets of classical separatist dualism so that we are in a position to contrast it with the integrative alternative.

According to the separatist interpretation, we were in a position to call it game, set, and match by the end of chapter 1. Just to prove the real distinction is the task of Descartes's dualism, and this is what we claimed to have accomplished. However, it now turns out that quite a few annotations need to be added to the proof, each glossing Descartes's understanding of the key notions involved: (i) the idea of a *real, complete subject* (substance)—both the mind and the body are meant to be such—and (ii) the idea of the kind of distinction involved when the relata are real subjects, a *real distinction*, so that DM and DB can each exist without the other.

Separatist Dualism I: Existential Separability

Separatist dualism demands that we read "can exist without the other" as a full-blown, real possibility—that is, it is really possible for DM to exist without DB; in turn, it is really possible for DB to exist without DM. A real distinction requires the real possibility of separate existence. However, in chapter 1, I argued that we may grant Arnauld his modal objection and assume modal inseparability of mind and body. "Can exist without the other," I assumed, was weaker, demanding mere consistency-with-what-DM-is rather than a real possibility for DM. In this respect, the framework of chapter 1 is an *attenuated* form of separatist dualism: we need not assume that conceivability of DM without DB entails a real possibility of DM without DB; we only assume that the conceivability entails the coherence of a story (model) with DM existing without DB.

Attenuated as our assumptions of chapter 1 are, the framework is that of separatist dualism: In some "locus" (a conceived story) respectful of what DM and DB are, DM *exists* without DB. It is in this last that an essential feature of separatist dualism lies: The separation of DM and DB rests ultimately on some such *existential* separability.

Separate Dualism II: Generic Essences

Existential separability is one fundamental feature of separate dualism. A second is the development of a *symmetric* account of the independence of mind and body.

As stated in chapter 1, in Meditation II (as in the treatise that underlies its metaphysics more theoretically, *The Principles of Philosophy*), there is a general tendency to specify very abstract and general whatnesses (essences). The human body ends up having as its nature—just like a stone, the Loire, or the Sun—the principal attribute of being extended. In a symmetric manner, the human mind is assigned this one principal attribute—it is a thinking thing. And so, even though the subtitle of Meditation II is "On the Nature of the Human Mind," by the time Descartes articulates the essence of this human mind, he does not mention that this mind of his is *of* a human being rather than of a Martian or an angel or a god.

This generic approach to the whatness of DM and DB calls for a finer formulation of one of our principles above, (iv), whatness separability. We should say that the separatist framework presupposed by our argument in chapter 1 asserted in effect two related principles concerning what DM and DB are:

(iv) Whatness separability: What DM is is distinct from what DB is.
(v) Generic whatness: The articulation of what DM and DB are—respectively, thinking and extended—is by means of generic, kind-blind attributes.

Separatist Dualism III: No Endurance Theory

The genericity of essence has so far shown in the absence of *inter*kind distinctions. For example, we find in Meditation II there is no separation in the essence of human, angelic, and divine minds; nor is there an intrinsic distinction among human, dog, and stone bodies. But the genericity of essence strikes a second time, this time at the *intra*kind level. Descartes's mind, DM, is one human mind; Plato's mind, PM, is another human mind. Asked to say when they existed, we would answer that the two existed at different times. Of course, we may (perhaps Descartes did) have a *theory* according to which both always existed and, for that matter, both still do. But I have not been asking about Descartes's theory, just about the natural answer to the question asked.

Given the disparate periods of existence, it is arguable (I, for one, would be happy to argue) that DM could not have existed at the time PM actually did; in turn, PM could not have existed in the first half of the seventeenth century. What is more, it may be argued that the manner and time in which DM came into being—by the coming into being of the *man* René Descartes—constrained the way in which it was possible for DM to change *while* in existence, during the 54 years it did exist between 1596 and 1650. It could thus be argued that DM could not have gone through its existence, enduring through a lifetime, in the manner actually gone through by PM, itself bound to the vicissitudes of that B.C. man Plato. In a nutshell, different human minds have essentially different possible lives, different possible *histories*. No explanation of such differences seems forthcoming from the generic essence theory, which assigns the same schematic essence—thinking thing—to both DM and PM.

What exactly is the problem here? First, a word about what problem is not raised by these endurance-in-time issues: I'm not worried here about "criteria of identity" for DM and PM. I stress this simply in view of the dominance in contemporary discussions of what are called "personal identity" theories. This vocabulary will make many readers surmise that I am lamenting here the absence of some such theory, multiplied by three—a theory of mind identity, body identity and personal (man) identity.

But this is not so. I am not driven by a quest for "criteria for identity"—be they for minds, bodies, or persons—a quest that dominates the practice of personal identity theories. Quite the opposite: I view it as an essential mark of everything real that it is governed by Bishop Butler's maxim that everything is what it is and not another thing, surely not a "definable thing," somehow reducible to its "criteria of identity," "necessary and sufficient conditions of identity," and other such individuation blueprints for being the distinct item one—mind, body, or person—is.

For Descartes, human minds and bodies (as well, as we shall see, human beings) are real subjects. As such, I believe that they escape reduction to criteria, definitions, and so on. I also believe that if Descartes were among us and aware of the dominance of such theories of criteria and defining conditions for real things, he would very much insist on the *in*definability of any real being simply because it is a *real* being.

So, my worry about the enduring DM and PM is not driven by the quest for criteria of identity. Rather my worry is that separatist dualism—with its generic essence assignment—forces a disjointed treatment of two questions that call for a unified account. The two questions concern (i) the whatness (essence) of a subject and (ii) its endurance in time.

We looked at the first question, the *whatness articulation* problem, in some detail in chapter 1 when we asked repeatedly about a variety of items: "What is this thing?" The second question, which has not so far been broached, concerns the endurance in time of real subjects. I call it the *lifetime description* problem. Existing in time—coming into history, changing in it, and coming to an end—is the mark of a real subject. Given such a subject, our metaphysics needs to describe what it took for this distinct thing to come to be, what sustained its changes, and what in the world had to happen for it to go out of existence.

Descartes was very much concerned with lifetime descriptions of subjects. For example, in Meditation II he provides a most abstract and generic discussion of the essence of various items, including a certain piece of wax. But even in this abstract and generic setting, he goes on to speculate not just about what this wax is but also about what is involved in its "remaining the same wax," what is involved in describing the wax's lifetime.

The trouble is that separatist dualism and its generic essence theory of mind and body—the former is thinking; the latter is extended—tells us nothing much about the lifetime description problem. For example, the two human minds DM and PM have different histories and endurance conditions, but nothing in the generic essence theory explains these differences—a silence that is even more troubling if we think of another mind, one that is internally similar to DM (e.g., a bundle of similar intellectual contents, or thoughts, as those had by DM). Call the mind DM* and make it exist in the body of a contemporary person, a man we shall call C. Obviously, DM* is an intellectual twin of that 400-years predecessor, DM. How are we to explain the noninternal differences in the lifetimes of these two minds? Similar worries may be raised for a contemporary twin body (DB*) of the 1651 dead-and-gone, original DB. Nothing in their common generic essence tells us about their distinct lifetime profiles.

This, then, is the concern about generic separatist dualism, a worry we shall attend to in some detail. At the moment, let us round up the exposition of separatist dualism by formulating this one last principle:

(vi) No endurance (lifetime description): The theory of generic essences (v) passes in silence over the endurance in time of DM and DB.[1]

Separatist Dualism IV: The Notion of Substance

The prove-too-little horn of our dilemma brings to the fore a fundamental feature of separatist dualism—its understanding of the idea of substance. The prove-too-little worry is this: Suppose we assume the primality of the human being and regard, in turn, the union between his mind, DM, and his body, DB, as in the very *nature* of such a mind and body. This is so because the very nature of each is now to be the mind and body of that primally given human being. It seems that we are on the verge of making the three of them—human mind, body, and being—three existentially interdependent substances. But to those familiar with classical glosses of the notion of substance—assumed by separatist dualism—this will seem to be a contradiction in terms: How can existentially interdependent items claim the rarefied title of a "complete thing," "substance," or "ens per se"? Is it not part of the very definition of a substance that it enjoys existential independence from all other beings (perhaps excepting the creator of them all)?

There is no doubt that Descartes speaks of "substance" in a separatist vein. But as prevalent in his writings is quite another

---

1. Let me add here a general remark, going beyond our strict Descartes agenda. The separation between personal identity problems and lifetime metaphysics questions strikes me as of general use. Personal (ship, bicycle, etc.) identity theories fuse in my view (i) atemporal (pseudo) issues about individuation and defining criteria with (ii) genuine lifetime (endurance) problems for individuals (with a given, primitive identity). In many of the genuine questions raised in personal identity puzzles, I find a quest for an explanation of the limits in the change potential of a specific item (René Descartes, the *Titanic*, etc.) of a specific kind (a person, a ship, etc.). More on the methodology of personal identity theories arises in chapter 3, in our discussions of illusions of conceivability.

conception of substance, and it is important to understand the difference. A striking encapsulation of this duality shows itself in Descartes's vacillation in his response to Arnauld (CSM II, 156–160), a text already discussed in detail throughout chapter 1.[2] In the space of four pages (CSM II, 156–160), the separatist idea shows up once and then very crisply: "The notion of substance is just this—that it can exist by itself, that is without the aid of any other substance."

This is stark enough. I would like to refer to the separatist idea of substance as *the existential conception*. We test for real subjecthood, because this is what real subjecthood *consists* of, by checking the existential profile of an item: Can it or can it not exist all by itself?

The potential for solitary existence is qualified when Descartes acknowledges the existential dependence of pure substances on God, their creator. But even with this qualification, the separatist's gloss of "substance" remains essentially existential—a sine qua non for an item's being a substance is its existential independence from every other thing but the divine.[3]

In the very same pages, we encounter another, *existence-free* notion of substance. The idea is that of (i) a subject of predication (ii) in which inhere attributes (modes), but (iii) it itself does not exist *in* a subject. This approach emphasizes what I call *categorical* facts about the candidate, facts relating to its profile in a "logical grammar" or in a theory of categories (types)—it is the subject of predication and itself is not one to

---

2. Concerning terminology: As we saw in the discussion of complete ideas in chapter 1, Descartes uses the two notions "substance" and "complete thing" interchangeably (see CSM II, 156, quoted in chapter 1). Even though I quote extensively in the section that follows, the reader may find it useful to have a copy of the fourth replies (CSM II, 156–160).

3. The only other place in these pages where the existence-involving notion is evoked is a bit later (CSM II, 160), when Descartes says in the arm-body passage already quoted: "And saying that the arm belongs to the nature of the whole man does not give rise to the suspicion that it cannot subsist in its own right."

be borne by subjects; it cannot be said to exist *in* subjects. I refer to this gloss of "substance" as *the categorical conception*.

When he introduces the idea of "complete thing," Descartes says:

> By a "complete thing" I simply mean a substance endowed with the forms or attributes which enable to recognize it as a substance. We do not have immediate knowledge of substances, as I have noted elsewhere. We know them only by perceiving certain forms or attributes which must inhere in something if they are to exist; and we call the thing in which they inhere a "substance." (CSM II, 156)

So far, this notion of substance is existence-free. Descartes goes on to apply this idea to the mind-body case:

> Just as being extendible and divisible and having shape etc. are forms or attributes by which I recognize the substance called body, so understanding, willing, doubting, etc. are forms by which I recognize the substance which is called mind. And I understand a thinking substance to be just much a complete thing as an extended thing. (CSM II, 156)

This is still free of any allusion to existential independence. The key continues to be the presence of a subject in which certain attributes inhere, the subject itself not existing in another subject as would an attribute or a mode.

At this point, Descartes reminds Arnauld that he, Descartes, has already articulated this (categorical) notion of substance elsewhere. One such venue is the gloss ("definition") in the geometrical exposition in the end of the second replies (CSM II, 114):

> Everything in which there exists immediately, as in a subject, or through which exists anything we perceive

that is any property, quality, or attribute of which a real idea is in us is called *substance*. Nor do we have any other idea of substance itself, precisely taken, than that it is a thing in which formally or eminently exists this something which we perceive, that is, which is objectively in some of our ideas, since it is known by the natural light that nothing can be a real attribute of nothing. (CSM II, 156)

Descartes also refers Arnauld back to the gloss in the first replies (CSM II, 86), where each of the real distincts has to be "an entity in its own right which is different from everything else" (CSM II, 156).

All of this glosses "substance" and "complete thing" in existence-free terms. This, then, is the second idea of Descartes. A substance is a subject of predication, in which we recognize both the inherence of a principal attribute—specifying the very kind of subject involved—and other properties (ways or modes) of the subject that are cast, in turn, as modes of that principal attribute. The attributes—principal or modifications—inhere in the substance; the substance itself does not exist in or through another subject. The substance is not a *way* of being; it is the *being* proper.[4]

We have before us the two conceptions, and I want to emphasize this one difference between them: To not exist in a subject does not imply the potential of solitary existence. In the categorical conception, a substance may be of necessity—stronger yet, by its very whatness—connected in its existence to other substances. All we are told by the categorical conception is that they—the candidate substances—do not exist *in* each other. The key to complete subjecthood is not existential independence but existence-as-a-subject and not in-a-subject.

---

4. Also in this vein are Descartes's remarks about "complete thing" to Caterus in the first replies, CSM II, 85–86.

From Real Subjects to Real Distinctions

In the categorical conception, we separate an *existential* real distinction from a real distinction *simpliciter*. A real distinction simpliciter is a distinction between two real subjects. This Descartes would like to contrast with a variety of other distinctions, such as between the subject and *its* modes or between two modes.

Suppose now our notion of a real subject is existential. Both DM and DB are, by hypothesis, real subjects. So, inasmuch as they are distinct at all, numerically distinct, it follows—on separatist lines of reasoning—that they are existentially separable from each other, that they could exist without the other. Of course, this does not settle the question of whether DM and DB, in the first place, make one thing or two. But we are required to admit as a necessary condition on their numerical distinction that they are existentially independent; of course, existential separability is assumed to be a *sufficient* condition for numerical distinction. Thus, the existential notion of substance engenders what we may call the idea of *existential real distinction*.

Suppose, on the other hand, that our notion of real subject is based on the categorical idea. Assume again that DM and DB are real subjects. Assume further that they are numerically distinct. Now, first, it is no longer required that they would be existentially separable, whether in a possibility or even merely in a conceived story. Second, there is nonetheless a sense of "real distinction" according to which the two may be really distinct. The sense is directly connected to the categorical sense of substance. The latter submits that to be such a substance is to be a subject of attributes and not to exist in a subject. The correlate idea of a *categorical real distinction* between x and y is that x and y are numerically distinct and each exists without existing in the other as in a subject. And so, for all that was said so far, it is quite conceivable that the human mind, body, and being are categorically really distinct from each other without being existentially really distinct.

2.3. Integrative Dualism: The Quest for Symmetry

A feature of separatist dualism emphasized above is its symmetric treatment of mind and body: Just as the essence of DB is free of any allusion to the human being whose body it is, the essence of DM is also free of reference to the man whose mind it is. In more general terms, the generic essence assignment is free of *human involvement*.

Integrative dualism casts itself at the outset as an opposite methodology. The ur-fact to be respected is that we are dealing with a man's mind and body. I refer to this basic fact as *the primality of the man*. I believe this one switch vis-à-vis separatist dualism is behind many others. But fundamental as the primality of the man is to integrative dualism, it confronts us with a textual mystery.

Descartes's writings include an explicit integrative proposal about the human body but not anything as direct about the human mind. A letter to Mesland in 1645, which we shall be looking at, offers clear blueprints for an integrative account of the human body. Some will doubt its authenticity, written as it was in a theological context. As mentioned at the outset, I am not a historian and will not engage in detective-like psychoanalysis of Descartes's "real" intentions. Whether he "really" intended its contents or not, the contents are crystal clear. And this is the problem—no equally explicit, integrative account of the human mind is suggested by Descartes.

Where are we to look then? Indirect indications of such an integrative account of the human mind are sown into Descartes's late essay *Passions of the Soul*. What is more, I argue that some fundamental features of Descartes's general metaphysics of substances—manifest already in Meditation II—lead us sooner or later, even in the case of human minds, to a theory of whatness and endurance in time that is in the integrative mold. And finally, since we speak of the letter to Mesland, it is even possible that enough is said there about

(M1) the endurance in time of objects in general (e.g., rivers)
(M2) the role of the mind in the endurance of the human body

to allow us to *infer* from (M1) and (M2) an integrative account of the human mind. Such an argument follows, but first let me reiterate the basic fact here: No matter how appealing the argument, there is nowhere in Descartes anything explicitly integrative about the mind, as there is in the Mesland letter about the human body.

This absence sets a task we may formulate as follows: How are we to reinstate, within the integrative framework, the mind-body symmetry manifested in separatist dualism? We may put the question this way: What would solve the following equation for Descartes?

$$\frac{\text{Separatist mind}}{\text{Separatist body}} = \frac{?}{\text{Integrative body (Mesland letter)}}$$

Integrative Dualism I: Bodies, Human and Other

My proposal is to investigate the letter of Mesland[5] with an eye to stating Descartes's account of what a human body is. With this much formulated, we may be clearer about what a symmetric—"integrative"—account of the human mind would come to:

> I consider what is the body of a man and I find that this word "body" is very ambiguous. When we speak in general of a body, we mean a determinate part of matter, a part of quantity of which the universe is composed. In this sense, if the smallest amount of that quantity were

---

5. Letter to Mesland, February 9, 1645. I was first made aware of this letter many years ago by a remark in a lecture of Rogers Albritton.

removed we would eo ipso judge that the body was smaller and no longer complete; and if any particle of the matter were changed we would at once think that the body was no longer quite the same, no longer *numerically the same*. But when we speak of the body of a man, we do not mean a determinate part of matter with a determinate size; we mean simply the whole of the matter joined to the soul of that man. And so, even though the matter changes, and its quantity increases or decreases, we still believe its the same body, *numerically the same*, provided that it remains joined in substantial union with the same soul; and we think that this body is whole and entire provided that it has in itself all the dispositions required to preserve that union. Nobody denies that we have the same bodies as we had in our infancy, although their quantity has much increased, and according to the common opinion of doctors, which is doubtless true, there is no longer in them any part of the matter which then belonged to them and even though they do not have the same shape any longer; so that they are only numerically the same because they are informed by the same soul. . . . Consequently, I do not think that there is any part of our bodies which remains numerically the same for a single moment, although our body, *qua* human body, remains always the same provided it is united with the same soul. In that sense, it can even be called indivisible; because if an arm or a leg of a man is amputated, we think that it is only in the first sense of "body" that his body is divided—we do not think that a man who lost an arm or leg is less a man than any other. Altogether then, provided that a body is united with the same rational soul, we always take it as the body of the same man whatever matter it may be and whatever quantity or shape it may have. (PL, 154–159)

This concerns the *human* body. The account of its existence through time, not in terms of some fixed quantity of matter, might be thought special to human bodies. But Descartes makes sure to stress a general metaphysical point earlier in the letter: "We can say that the Loire is the same river as it was ten years ago, although it is not the same water, and perhaps there is no longer a single part left of the earth which surrounded that water" (PL, 156).

I isolate in these passages two themes that will play a central role in the integrative picture. The first concerns the metaphysics of bodies (objects) in general—rivers, pieces of wax, and human bodies—and their endurance in time. The second point concerns specifically the identity of human bodies and what it takes for one to endure through change. I consider first the specific human body claim. The general metaphysics of enduring objects will concern us later.

Generic Bodies: Descartes Cuts

In the first sentence of the passage, Descartes alludes to an ambiguity in the concept of "body":

> When we speak in general of a body, we mean a determinate part of matter, a part of quantity of which the universe is composed. In this sense, if the smallest amount of that quantity were removed we would eo ipso judge that the body was smaller and no longer complete. (PL, 156)

This is also the notion assumed by the separatist treatment of body-in-general in Meditation II.[6] I see it as marked by six fundamental theses:

(SDB1)   *Ontological primality:* DB, simply qua body, is ontologically primal; the human being RD—the entity composed from it and DM—is derivative in its con-

---

6. CSM II, 17.

ditions of (i) existence, (ii) identity, and (iii) articulation of what it is.

(SDB2) *Essence:* The essence of DB is generic; what-it-is is an extended thing.

(SDB3) *Existence:* DB's existence, simply qua body, does not depend on the existence of the man, RD.

(SDB4) *Endurance:* The instantaneous conception of body, for example, of DB, does not allow for *its* endurance through change.

(SDB5) *Substance:* DB is a substance in the sense of existential independence.

(SDB6) *Real distinction:* DB is really distinct from the man RD (and from the mind DM) in the existential sense—it can exist without RD and without DM.

The key theses are (SDB1) and (SDB2). By (SDB1), DB is given prior to and independently of its eventual contribution to the making of that derivative entity, the human being RD. The separatist picture is of bodies and minds created separately and leading their autonomous existence. The notion of a human being—whether the result of a compounding, composition, or union of a mind and a body—is just this: a subsequent binding of antecedently given mind and body. In particular, in itself, DB is *just* a material body—a cluster of matter or an extension—not the body of an entity of a certain kind (a human body), let alone the body of a *specific* entity of a given kind (the body of this human being RD).

This conception is further articulated in (SDB2). The essence of DB is said to be exhausted by the generic attribute—it is an extended thing. For all that its generic essence specifies, DB could very well be the body of another human being, for example, Princess Elizabeth; and with equal ease, it could be the body of an entity of quite a different kind, the body of a giraffe or a statue.

Thus, DB is given as an instantaneous cut, a distribution of matter in space. The slightest alteration in the material composition leads to another such instantaneous body. I call this definition by abstraction of a body the postulation of a *Descartes cut*: Corresponding to every three-dimensional, instantaneous cut in the material composition of the universe, we postulate a body.[7]

The remaining principles (SDB3)–(SDB6) fall into place once we read them as intended for Descartes cuts. For its existence, the instantaneous cut does not depend on this specific human being RD, "constructed" from it and other such cuts. Similarly, this body, given strictly as a simple cluster of matter, is not a real historical subject—one that comes into being in time, changes through time, and eventually comes to an end. Finally, a body may be viewed as a substance when we classify by the existential conception assumed by the separatist. Each such Descartes cut owes its existence to the cut definition and not to any robust metaphysical connections with other real historical objects.

Bodies of a Given Kind

The preceding discussion articulates the conception of body Descartes relies on throughout Meditation II. What is striking about the letter to Mesland is that Descartes sketches a second conception of the human body—indeed, of other kinds of bodies, for example, rivers. This alternative conception is not merely intriguing for its consequences concerning the mind-body question. As mentioned, it lays out a substantially different metaphysics of objects in general. I see this second conception, when applied to DB, as characterized by a corresponding sextet of theses:

(IDB1)   *Ontological primality:* The human being, for example, RD, is the entity in terms of which it is speci-

---

7. My terminology is meant to remind us of a mathematical analogy from a procedure of Dedekind in which for each "cut" in the system of rational numbers, we postulate the existence of a real number.

fied what DB is, that is, the body of a man. Consequently, the conditions of (i) existence and (ii) identity of DB are specified in terms of the man whose body it is.

(IDB2) *Essence:* DB is assigned a full-blooded essence—the body of a human being.

(IDB3) *Existence:* DB existentially depends on RD (and vice versa); in turn, it depends on DM.

(IDB4) *Endurance:* DB is a historical subject, enduring through change of material composition.

(IDB5) *Substance:* DB is a substance in the categorical sense—a subject of a category of predications; it itself is not a mode or way of being of a subject.

(IDB6) *Real distinction:* DB is really distinct, in the categorical—if not the existential—sense, from RD (and, in turn, from DM).

Yet again, the key lies in the first two theses. Throughout his letter, Descartes emphasizes the contrast between thinking of a body abstractly ("in general") and taking it as the body of "a man," indeed, of a specific historical subject of this kind, a man with a particular history. Taken in the latter way, the body has this "of-ness" built into what-it-is: It is the body of a human being. We are no longer given an array of "generic bodies" and "generic minds," only to fancy ourselves creative architects who are to construct from them an array of human beings. We start with a given human being and ask about *its* body a variety of metaphysical questions: What is the nature of this body, the kind of item it is? Under what conditions can it come into existence? What does it take for it to endure through change? Finally, what among bodies of its kind distinguishes it as this specific one?

The key answer is the one about whatness. What DB is is a human body; this is glossed as the body of a human being. There is a latent ambiguity in this last claim because of the indefinite article: For example, is DB the body of some human being or other ("any old human being")? Or is it essentially the body of a specific human being, say, RD?

The intended answer is based on the home truth that Descartes's body, DB, and Elizabeth's body, EB, are the *same kind* of object—a human body. Suppose we allowed in the whatness-specifying statement a reference to the particular man, René Descartes: What DB is is the body of this man, RD. Thus, DB and EB would no longer share whatness. This seems to be an error: DB and EB are the same kind of thing, a human body. Which body, among human bodies, is DB? The body of René Descartes. This is true of DB throughout its lifetime and in any counterfactual possibility. It is also individuative of DB among its kind—no other human body is René Descartes's body. But when it comes to what DB is—the kind of item it is—it is just what EB is, a human body.[8]

The primality of man encoded into (IDB1) and (IDB2) impinges on existence questions broached in (IDB3). The existence of the body is subordinated to that of the man: When the man dies, its living human body is dead and gone; the remaining alignment of molecules on the pathologist's table is—despite its being the same material extension as before—another kind of thing, a corpse. Thus, as urged in (IDB4), DB has been transformed from a generic abstraction—an instantaneous distribution of matter in space—into a historical subject, one that is generated in history, undergoes change, survives material alterations in composition, and eventually corrupts when the man whose body it is has come to an end. Finally, (IDB5) and

---

8. This view precludes the possibility—in actual or counterfactual history—that this body, DB, will "become" the body of a man other than Descartes. And given a certain man, say, René Descartes, it precludes its coming to have any other body than DB. This pits the present metaphysics against more modern, neo-Lockean theories of "personal identity." The alleged possibilities of man-body swaps allowed by such modern views are discussed in detail in chapter 3. I also return there to the important question of whether what DB is is not just the body of a man but also the body of this particular man, Descartes.

(IDB6) insist on an alternative sense in which DB is a substance; DB has now been made existentially dependent on two others—RD and DM. But it is the distinct subject of predications, including the previously mentioned changes in predicates across time. And although it is the subject of predications, it itself does not exist in others—for example, in DM or in RD—as a predicate inheres in a subject; it is, rather, a subject whose existence is interdependent on the existence of these other subjects. Consequently, DB is really distinct from RD (and, in turn, DM) in the categorical sense—both relata of the distinction relation are subjects, and neither exists in the other as a property inheres in a subject.

Integrative Dualism II: The Human Mind

The subtitle of Meditation II is "On the Nature of the Human Mind." But soon enough the account turns out to be of mind in general, notwithstanding any allusion to the kind of mind it is. We have seen that in the letter to Mesland, Descartes provides a nongeneric account of both the man and its human body, both treated as real, historical subjects. The question is what account of the man's mind would fit into this second approach.

One qualification is called for at the outset. It could be argued that for all that Descartes *literally* says in the letter, the account of mind suggested may be taken in the generic way. Descartes speaks of the human body as being the same as long as it remains united to the same mind. This remark seems to imply that the mind itself endures in time—*remains* the same: The body remains united to the same mind by remaining united to a mind that remained the same. But even in such a reading, it is still possible to give quite an abstractionist account of mind. For example, the enduring mind in question need not be specified as a mind of a human being: Might not my human body be informed through and through by an angelic mind?

In a more general way, we may frame a consistent reading of the Mesland letter by proposing a theory of whatness and endurance for minds that does not account for them as intrinsically *human* minds. Here we are only to recall the "ambiguity" in the notion of body that Descartes points out in the first line of the quotation on page 72 (PL, 156). That is, we may contemplate a symmetric "ambiguity" in the notion of mind.

Consider the generic idea of mind, mind "in general." This idea is not a mere hypothetical analog of the body-in-general idea of the Mesland letter. It is the actual idea of mind proposed by Descartes in Meditation II (CSM II, 18–19). The conception is laid out in the paragraphs following Descartes's decision to shift from the primal question "What am I?" to "What is mind?" All we have to do now is reconsider the separatist body principles (SDB1)–(SDB6), except one (which we shall discuss shortly), and make the obvious substitutions. We have before us the principles that characterize the separatist conception of mind:

(SDM1) *Ontological primality.* DM, simply qua mind, is ontologically primal; the human being RD—the entity composed from it and DB—is derivative in its conditions of (i) existence, (ii) identity, and (iii) articulation of what it is.

(SDM2) *Essence.* The essence of DM is generic; what-it-is is a thinking thing.

(SDM3) *Existence.* DM's existence, qua mind, does not depend on the existence of the man, RD.

(SDM5) *Substance.* DM is a substance in the sense of existential independence.

(SDM6) *Real distinction.* DM is really distinct from RD and DB in the existential sense—it can exist without them.

One principle is missing, (SDM4), which concerns endurance in time. An account of mind-in-general that is fully symmetric to the body-in-general idea of the Mesland letter would insist on the analog principle (SDM4):

(SDM4) *Endurance.* The instantaneous conception of mind, for example, of DM, does not allow for *its* endurance through change.

As we shall see in a moment, there is no way of reading Meditation II's generic account of mind as subscribing to this principle. The nontransfer of this one separatist principle challenges reflection. What if Descartes were not wholly separatist about minds after all?

2.4. Subjects in Time: Two Cartesian Frameworks

The materials that make up the instantaneous notion of body in the Mesland letter are "physical" (a cluster of particles, an assortment of physical qualities of the extension, etc.). The analog—an instantaneous mind—would be yet again a kind of Descartes cut, but this time of intellectual ingredients: an instantaneous cut of thoughts and willings. The materials, or fabrics, that make up instantaneous bodies and minds are different; logically, the conception is the same, that is, composition from the relevant instantaneous "parts."

The slightest change in composition—intellectual or physical—would give us a different item: mind or body. In both cases, we do not have real, historical subjects that are generated in time, endure in history, and eventually corrupt. Rather, we have abstractions, with fixed identities imposed on logical grounds by the cut definitions and excluding by fiat any survival through alteration of qualities.[9]

---

9. I speak here of a bundle of purely intellectual ingredients because in various contexts Descartes asserts that perceptual, imaginative, and affective states require essentially the existence of a body (note that in an existen-

The conception of mind as a bundle of intellectual qualities is interesting; variations on the theme have been alluded to by eminent readers of Descartes (most famously, Hume, but also Locke and modern personal identity theorists). But no matter how generic the other principles of Meditation II are about mind, Descartes himself does not endorse this last analogy concerning endurance in time. For Descartes, a given human mind is never analyzed as an instantaneous bundle of intellectual qualities; a specific human mind is an enduring subject. A given human mind can change and remain numerically the same mind—different thoughts but still the same mind. When Hume, Locke, and Kant pursue a culprit that so sustains ("blunders into") the existence of a mysterious inner subject, it is Descartes they are after.

This suggests that if any body, any "physicalia," of Meditation II is to serve as a model for Descartes's conception of a given human mind, the item may not be the abstractly given instantaneous body (extension). Rather, it should be a robustly given item, constantly changing in history. Such an item does come up for dissection in Meditation II. It is the piece of wax (first appearing in CSM II, 20–21).

The (piece of) wax is brought to the fore late in Meditation II as a "simplified case" for an analogy when we frame our account of the human mind. This much is not in dispute. What is more controversial is the "dimension" over which the piece of wax is to serve as a "model" for the human mind. But before I take a stand here, I must note a simple fact, one holding for various interpretations of the piece-of-wax-as-a-model: Side by

---

tially separatist notion of a substance, this dependence would endanger the substancehood of the mind). Thus, it is somewhat surprising to find Descartes himself, in the Synopsis to his Meditations, mention "desires" and "sensations" in a context relevant to the present discussion (see CSM II, 10). Perhaps he relates to the purely intellectual aspect of a desire. In this discussion, I assume that the ingredients, for example, thoughts, that "make up" an instantaneous mind need nothing but God to exist.

side with the abstractionist, ahistoric account of bodies, Descartes's discussion of the changing wax in Meditation II shows a keen interest in a metaphysics of robust historical subjects that endure in time.

The side-by-side presence of two opposite outlooks strikes me as a general problem in Descartes's metaphysics, even before we come to the particular case of human minds. In different contexts and sometimes in a single, broad context (e.g., Meditation II), Descartes operates with two competing conceptions of objects ("substances"), their essence (whatness) and their endurance in time. To reiterate, the ambiguity and/or ambivalence cuts across the board, applying to all kinds of subjects—pieces of wax, rivers, human bodies, and (purported subjects that they are) human minds.

Consider rivers, for example, Descartes's Loire. By the cut definition, we fix on a certain set of earth-and-water particles at a given time. There now follows an abstractionist theory of essence (what-it-is), numerical identity, and existence in time. For essence, we are merely told the very abstract and generic: It is an extended object. For identity, the Descartes cut slices the object as thinly as possible: Any variation in the quality set gives us another object. Finally, for endurance, there is no enduring in time for *this* object, as the water flows and the river bank erodes, and so on. All in all, the whatness, individuation, and endurance conditions abstract from the robust historical subject, the Loire-through-the-ages. We are given a "logical object," an abstraction.

This project of Descartes involves a form of *subspecies-aeternitate* metaphysics. The metaphysician is not operating "from below," from inside the muck of things; he is not describing the life of *this* body and *this* mind, let alone *this man* they make up. Nor is it his or her task to account for the evolution in history of *this* river and *this* piece of wax. The project is rather to classify everything whatsoever by a simple system of genera (a "two-sorted logic" would have said the modern logician): extended vs. thinking. The metaphysician is operating "from above," really from beyond the cosmological receptacle within which things are endowed with a specific history and are members of specific kinds. I call this project of describing the whole world "from above" Descartes's *abstractionist metaphysics*.

I call the kind of second project Descartes is interested in *lifetime metaphysics* because here our focus is on describing, from inside the cosmos, the lifetimes of specific historical items, what it takes for them to come to be and the limits of change they can endure. For essence, instead of the generic, two-sorted classification (extended vs. thinking), objects are now subsumed in specific kinds—rivers, pieces of wax, stones, human minds, angelic minds, and divine minds. When it comes to individuation, each such object is not reduced to this or that cut of qualities; the qualities are simply borne by the object.

There is now, at least logically, the potential for an alteration of qualities that preserves the identity of the pertinent objects such as the piece of wax or the Loire. By *logical potential* I mean to indicate this: It might still turn out that, in the cosmos, things are so organized that no object ever alters its qualities. But if, indeed, each object is changeless, this would not be due to a "from above" logical doctrine about identity that stipulated the result; rather, it would be due to the fact that, metaphysically, this is the way things stand in the world.

This potential for logical change is accorded to all mundane objects. It is realized in different ways by different objects, depending on the kind of objects they make. To bring out *the metaphysical potential* of a specific object, we engage in its lifetime description—how items of its kind actually evolve and how, at different points in the object's history, it *might have* gone on to be. We thus discover different metaphysical potentials—to a specific whatness belongs a specific manner of preserving it as time goes by; rivers are rivers, wax is wax.

As I read him, Descartes is interested in two different projects in metaphysics. Our task, therefore, is to keep his distinct projects separate. When providing a lifetime metaphysics for the human being and his body, Descartes puts behind him the abstractionist account of body and calls on his robust metaphysics of enduring items. My suggestion is that a similar move is needed in the case of the human mind for two reasons. First, to make sense of what Descartes says of the human body, if the mind is to continually "inform" the enduring body, keep it and the human being whose body it is *living*, we can no longer rely on a generic-abstractionist conception of mind; we need to treat the mind as a historical subject, evolving with this human body. Moreover, we need to understand this coevolution as determined by the kinds of items the evolving subjects are—a *human* mind and body (the coevolution of other symbiotic duos, e.g., binary stars or pairs of elementary particles would proceed differently). Second, quite apart from the Mesland letter, which is focused on the "informing"-the-body role—that is, just thinking of the mind by itself—we need to account for its intellectual *life*: the changes in content ("I have just changed my mind") as it remains one and the same mind.

It is my suggestion, then, to start in Meditation II with what Descartes says about a perfectly mundane item, the piece of wax, which he intends to be a simplified model for the case of the human mind. We must understand what in his metaphysical dynamics is the basis for the wax's enduring through change; then, with this model before us, we must reflect on what it takes another enduring subject, DM, to persist through change.

Subjects in Time I: The Enduring Piece of Wax

What does Descartes tell us about the piece of wax in Meditation II?[10] It is a cluster of epistemological issues that has drawn attention in the wax discussion. How do we track this item as it changes and how do we come to know its essence? But our

---

10. In what follows, when I speak of "the wax passage" I refer to CSM II, 20–21.

focus here is the metaphysical question: What in the world grounds this item's endurance through change?

We need a name for our piece of wax. Introducing it, Descartes tells us, "It has just been taken from the honeycomb," and so I shall refer to it as Hon. Descartes tells us that after being warmed up and melted down, Hon has changed radically, losing many of its original, sensible qualities. The qualities it has kept are "extendible, changeable, flexible." The trio of qualities is Descartes's official proposal for the essence of Hon. Descartes also repeatedly uses the phrase "it remains the same wax." Of course, he wants to indicate the stable numerical identity of what he calls "one particular body," that is, Hon. In so referring to Hon, however, he not only assures us that it has persisted in being one and the same entity but he also concedes that it has remained through and through of the same kind—wax. So, in my reading, being-a-piece-of-wax is also a persisting property of Hon. In all, Descartes tells us that throughout the wax's shedding of its sensible qualities, there stably remains one and the same individual item (Hon) of the same kind of stuff (wax).

A friend of Descartes's abstractionist metaphysics might well object at this point in the following way:

> For all that was said so far, Descartes need not call on a lifetime metaphysics of enduring objects to get a complete description of the changes that have occured in the pertinent part of the world. He should rather describe things in this way: Having warmed up a certain Descartes cut, a definite body extension (Hon), we have affected that item's shape. As a result, we drove this extension out of existence. The resulting melted-down item (call it Mel) is a new Descartes cut, another body viz. another extension. Sure enough, the changes have been continuous and have followed a familiar path of chemical deformation. But when we remind ourselves that each body is "a determinate part of matter, a part of

quantity of which the universe is composed," we see that the warming up of Hon has given us another body-object. The fact that the change between Hon and Mel seems continuous enough is what lies at our inclination to posit a single enduring object. But, strictly, all that has happened to the world is that one extension—a given cluster of matter—was replaced by another. Proceeding in this way, we could give a complete description of the history of the world, the changes that colloquially we would describe as incurring in Hon and in the Loire and in my lifelong human body.

The objection claims that we could proceed—with pieces of wax, as with rivers and human bodies—without a dynamics of enduring objects. Could we?

Possibly—or so at least we are told by many metaphysicians, ancient and modern, from Heraclitus to Quine, all weary of our marketplace descriptions in terms of enduring objects. Now, my task in this book is not to evaluate the correctness of this "anything you (marketplace man) could do, I (abstractionist metaphysician) could do (better)." My focus is on understanding Descartes. Given the two metaphysical schemes he operated with, he surely had the means to issue such a theoretical-physicist "could describe the world" claim. He could so describe the wax and the Loire and the human body. But he did not. In describing the changes from the warming up of the wax, he used the language of the marketplace—as changes *in* the enduring Hon. And here lies our question: What facts about Hon ground this marketplace description?

My hypothesis is that it all turns on the essence of Hon, on what-it-is. Make its whatness generic, and persistence through change is not open to it. In contast, accord Hon robust whatness, and you have endowed it with a real potential for change. We might summarize the basic hypothesis:

(E)   No endurance without robust whatness.

My reasoning about Descartes is this: He describes Hon as enduring; by principle (E), he must view it as having a robust whatness.

Indeed, he does. Descartes emphasizes that the wax stays throughout "extendable, changeable and flexible." But he also stresses—by repeatedly *using* the phrase "remains the same wax"—that through and through Hon remains the same kind of thing, that is, a piece of *wax*. The limits of change that Hon can endure rest very much on this last attribution: For example, Hon may not change into a piece of gold; nor could some initial piece of gold change into Hon. The process of warming up and expanding in extension as described by Descartes pertains to wax: At the temperatures described, our candidate piece of gold (Goldie) would not have melted at all. At temperatures at which Goldie would have melted, the waxness of Hon would have long been destroyed and, with it, Hon itself. The motion of the particles inside the wax molecules would be high enough to dismantle the chemical composition that is a sine qua non for being beeswax—$C_{30}H_{61}OCOC_{15}H_{31}$. On the other hand, Goldie, being made of a heavy atomic element, is subject to different procedures: To melt *it* down, let alone to break up the gold atoms that it is made of, quite a different chemical reaction is necessary.

Such are the differences at the "corruption" stage. There are correlate differences in their respective "generation." Hon and Goldie must have followed different processes of coming to be. Hon was just drawn from the honeycomb. Ordinary earthly temperatures permit the breeding of that kind of stuff. But golden stuff—recall that the atom is one of the heavier elements—could not get going in the honeycomb. It took rather dramatically high temperatures in the interior of stars to engender atoms of that kind.

In sum, suppose we describe the two pieces of matter in front of us—Hon and Goldie—in merely generic terms as "extended things." There is very little we can do to describe their distinct profiles of persistence in time in a natural way. For all that is said under the generic description, someone—a philosophical alchemist—can attempt to convert the one into the other; there is nothing to block the transformation of (what we, from the outside, using kind terms would describe as) a piece of gold-at-t into a piece of wax-at-t'.

This result is forthcoming for two, seemingly opposite metaphysical theories that are abstractionist in their approach to Hon and Goldie. One is Descartes's own theory of identifying individuals with their Descartes cuts and more generally, an item with its "bundle of qualities." The second theory seems to be at the other end of the metaphysical spectrum; that is, each such individual—like Hon and Goldie—is a "bare particular," with no property whatsoever pertaining to its essence or what it is. For that matter, the particular could be made "almost bare," with "extended" forming the sole property pertaining to its nature. The two pictures might seem radically different, the first canonizing every property of Hon and Goldie as a sine qua non for being-it, the second denying any property that title. But, in truth, the two outlooks are variations on a common theme—abstraction from the robust historical individual. The one picture abstracts the bundle of qualities, the other some imaginary pointlike subject. In so abstracting, both blur the fundamental distinction between *what* the mundane individual is and features pertaining merely to *how* things stand with it at the instant of abstraction.

Suppose, then, that we abstract from the facts as follows:

(Kind)   The kind of thing Hon is is a piece of wax; the kind of thing Goldie is is a piece of gold.

By abstracting (Kind), we have now "homogenized" Hon and Goldie. As two pointlike bare subjects, they can come to bear any properties whatsoever; as two Descartes cuts, they cannot change at all. Either way, we do not get the natural description of two lifetimes of change, for example, the one Descartes himself provides for Hon.

Subjects in Time II: The Enduring Human Mind

What is good for the wax is good for the human mind, or so says Descartes's *the wax-as-a-model principle*. Most often the principle is applied in relation to the epistemology of essence. In such applications, we ask: By what mental faculty and kind of data do we get to know the essence of a given subject? The wax is then deployed to illustrate the proposal that it is the pure intellect, not the senses, that reveals to us what the wax is. We are now urged by the wax-as-a-model principle to project the result to the manner in which the essence of the mind is to be divulgated.

In contrast, our present application is throughly metaphysical. With Hon, we reasoned as follows: Descartes allows it to endure through change; there is no endurance without robust whatness; thus, he must be endowing Hon with a robust whatness. I propose the same line of reasoning for the human mind. Our example of a specific mind is, as before, Descartes's mind, DM.

Descartes tells us at the outset, in the synopsis of the Meditations, that DM and its kind are subjects of change: "Even if all the accidents of the mind change, so that it has different objects of the understanding, and different desires and sensations, it does not on that account become a different mind" (CSM II, 10). Descartes emphasizes later, in Meditation II (CSM II, 18–19) that, as he sleeps and awakes, perceives and daydreams, walks and thinks, one and the same human mind remains.

Meditation VI and his fourth replies to Arnauld add important facts about the enduring linkage of this given mind and its sustaining body. We find that DM is not linked to DB as a "pilot to a ship." Such a hookup would have been forged rather late in the life of both relata. The linkage is rather to be thought of—according to Descartes's fourth replies (CSM II, 160)—on the model of the hookup of Descartes's arm (DA) with DB. This relation is part of the very coming into being of both relata and is in the very—I am using Descartes's word—*nature* of both. In Meditation VI, Descartes goes on to speculate on *where*, in the human body, the relation is based. It is in the pineal gland (*conarion*) that a lifelong dynamics of back-and-forth "information transfer" occurs: The mind gets its information from the senses and the brain and instructs them about actions to be taken.[11]

I want to emphasize that what is up for evaluation here is not a matter of correctness—does the conarion hypothesis reveal to us what the union between mind and body is really like? Rather, our objective is a better grasp of Descartes's conception of the modalities of the connection. He tells us that it is written into the *nature* of a human mind to be, throughout its life, in union with a given body that it informs. The accidents of the body to which it is connected will change as it—the mind—goes through life; so will the intellectual accidents of the mind proper. But throughout, we will have only one mind and one body interconnected.

Subjects in Time III:
The Abstractionist's Challenge

So far, Descartes provides, as with the wax, marketplace descriptions of a single human mind that is enduring through both bodily and intellectual changes. Is this form of description inevitable? The description in terms of a single subject that is enduring through change has been challenged in the case of the wax by the abstractionist metaphysician. Reasoning by Descartes's own wax-as-a-model principle, various philosophical readers of Descartes—most notably Locke—turn the tables against him: What is good for the wax, is good for the mind; no endurance metaphysics is called for the wax and thus none for the human mind. The challenge runs like this: To explain "the lifetime of a mind," there is no need to posit the mind as

11. CSM II, 59–60.

an enduring substance. A succession of momentary minds, properly strung to preserve memories and other "telling" experiential facts would do just as well.

Among philosophers who argue in this vein, there are different emphases on the sense in which such a situation is "indistinguishable" from the enduring subject assumed by marketplace descriptions. To some, the point concerns the epistemology of the situation viewed *from the outside*: I, an external observer, would not be wiser if the man I observe, René Descartes, were sustained in time not by the single persisting DM but by a succession of momentary minds. To other philosophers, the point concerns the epistemology of the situation viewed *from the inside*: Descartes himself—relying on his inner feeling of what it is like, as well as introspection—would not be wiser if God were to revolve a succession of momentary minds inside his head instead of the single, lifelong DM. To yet a third group of philosophers, the point intended here concerns both outside and inside epistemology: There is simply no standpoint from which we could tell the operation of an enduring-mind hypothesis from the sequence of the momentary minds counterpart.

I suspect that all three groups leap from these epistemic observations—right or wrong as they might be about how things would appear—to metaphysical conclusions about the kind of facts necessary to describe the life of René Descartes. As emphasized, the leap is not special to the case of the mind. It is based on the methodology relied on when the issue is the prerequisites of a complete description of the piece of wax, the Loire, or the human body. In my understanding, what is being assailed by Locke is not essentially and distinctly the case of the human mind as a subject of change but the very methodology of positing enduring subjects of change.

As emphasized in our discussion of the wax and the Loire, our task here is not to join this metaphysical dispute by evaluating the abstractionist's challenge. Our task is to understand Descartes. There is not much of a question about what language of description he adopts. Descartes, who uses a dynamic metaphysics for pieces of wax, rivers, and human bodies, emphatically proposes such a lifetime metaphysics for human minds. The question before us is rather this: What facts according to Descartes's lifetime metaphysics endow the human mind with its change potential?

As before, it all turns on what the essence of our subject is. Make DM's essence generic—merely a "thinking thing"—and the endurance metaphysics is jeopardized. Make the whatness robust—the mind of a given human being—and change is not only possible for it but also necessary for its own lifelong survival. Of course, in the context of his generic metaphysics, Descartes is famous for assigning DM the mere "thinking thing" as its generic whatness. But in the setting of his lifetime metaphysics, a robust whatness is called on. It is to this robust essence for DM that we now turn.[12]

Subjects in Time IV: Three Lifetime Principles

Descartes submits that throughout the wax's shedding of its sensible qualities, there remains one and the same individual item (Hon); it stably remains of the same kind of stuff it was (wax). With DM, we are told the same: Throughout its changes of desires and thoughts, there stably remains one and the same individual item (DM) and one the same kind of item (a human mind). But there is more: Throughout the changes, it stably remains true that DM is the mind of the same human being.

This third stable feature—DM is always the mind of the same human being—I call *the prime lifetime fact* because it is

---

12. Related to the robustness of essence is what the metaphysician would assert to be conceivable. Many in the generic essence tradition have argued that they can conceive for DM a variety of body-shedding scenarios. In contrast, a robust essence of DM exposes such claims of conceivability as unfounded, if we read them as de re conceivings, that is, scenarios for this specific item, DM. I dwell on this difference in chapter 3.

the most fundamental fact in Descartes's account of the life of a mind like DM. I see the prime lifetime fact as encapsulating three principles in one claim.

The first principle proposed here is that the kind of mind a mind is is stable in time. Given that DM is a *human* mind, it may not turn into an angelic or divine mind. And thus we have

(Stability)   The kind of a mind is lifetime stable.

Second, we get a principle about kind subsumption. Consider, for example, the body of a dog. It is natural to propose that a body is a dog body iff it is the body of a dog being, that is, of a dog. The principle suggested for minds is a natural generalization:

(Of-ness)   A mind is of a given kind iff it is the mind of a being of that kind.

Thus, the kind of a mind is the very kind of the being whose mind it is. So, to be a human rather than an angelic or a divine kind of mind, DM is through and through the mind of a human being.[13]

For its whole lifetime, DM is stably a human mind; and, moreover, the mind of a human being. Which one? Here enters the third and last principle packed into the prime lifetime fact, a principle about the counting of individual human minds:

(One-One)   One mind, one man; one man, one mind.

The one-one principle tells us that given a certain mind—say, DM—there is throughout its lifetime only one human being

---

13. A symmetric of-ness principle was seen to govern, in the letter to Mesland, human bodies. What makes DB throughout its life a human body is that it is the body of a human being.

(and by Mesland's letter, human body) it informs. By this principle (if not by the previous two), the familiar philosophical fantasies (which, alas, since Locke dominate the subject called "personal identity") of mind swapping between two humans are ruled out. That is, DM may not turn into the mind of Princess Elizabeth; her mind, EM, cannot become René Descartes's mind.

It should also be noted that the one-one principle is unitarian in the opposite direction. Given a certain human being—say René Descartes—he may have throughout his life only the mind (and body) he was engendered with; he may get perhaps another arm or leg, but when it comes to his mind it is the original or nothing.[14]

We may well appreciate that these three foregoing principles—stability, of-ness, and one-one—are not natural in the generic whatness conception. Let DM's essence be simply "a thinking thing." First, there is nothing now to block DM's becoming the mind of an angel; in essence, angel Gabriel's mind and DM are alike. Second, there is nothing to force of-ness on DM. The nature of the mind is not determined by the specific kind of being whose mind it is. Rather, the nature of the mind is determined first, generically, as it were, as a thinking thing. Its serving as the thinking apparatus of a human being is part of the historical vicissitudes befalling that already essentially determined mind.

Third, in the generic conception the one-one principle is obviously false. One, starting with a given mind, it is conceiv-

---

14. Some modern anti-Lockean theorists of personal identity find attractive an analogous view about the brain. The attractiveness is independent of whether one also holds the further reductive thesis that the mind is identical to the brain. I, for one, would hold with Descartes that my mind and brain are two subjects. But I would also hold with Descartes the integrative dualist that both abide by the one-one principle. Such intuitions about the brain suggest, as mentioned above, that Descartes would have been better off using the brain-body rather than arm-body model in his fourth replies.

able that this thinking thing becomes the thinking unit of another man-body unit. And easy to conceive or not, there is surely nothing in the nature of the mind to tie it to the particular human being in which it started its life (assuming it is only then that the mind's life started, an assumption many a separatist dualist denies). Two, given a certain human being, it is readily conceivable—recall again the familiar philosophical fantasies—that this body would be run by another thinking thing, a different pilot for the same ship.[15]

In closing, we may summarize the difference between the abstractionist and lifetime theories of essence in the following terms. The abstractionist begins by abstracting from the real man—from that real individual and from the specific real kind of being it is. The basic ingredients we start with are a mind, a thinking thing, and a body, an extended thing. Inasmuch as a man emerges, it is the result of a subsequent hookup of these two ingredients. This late linkage lends credibility to the idea that the man's mind can be conceived without his body and vice versa; it also lends credibility to the assertion that one can exist without the other.

The integrative outlook begins with the real human being. The quest is to better understand the primal answer (a man) to the primal question (What am I?). It turns out that such an understanding must proceed in two stages. First, we are being shown that inside each such real man, a human mind and body

---

15. This concerns the classical separatist conception. A variation on it goes like this: The freedom of mind swapping is accorded to a given human *body* and *being* but not to a *person*. In this variant separatist picture, the identity of the person is given in terms of his or her mind, whose identity is specified independently and does not depend on that of the human being. What is more, in this picture, unlike the integrative picture that emerges from the letter to Mesland, a person may associate in a lifetime with many different (human) bodies and beings. Such accounts are suggested by the "personal identity" literature, which I discuss in detail in chapter 3.

must be discerned. Second, having ascertained this distinction, we are shown how the mind and body are integrated inside that primal item, the man. Nowhere along the proof of the distinction do we forget where we came from; that is, we never abstract so much that we forget that the mind and body we are to distinguish are (i) a *human* mind and body and, moreover, (ii) of a particular human being, for example, RD.

The kinds of mind and body we are operating with are essential from the outset: They are those of a man. This sets the limits for what changes either can endure in two ways. First, just as we get restrictions from the fact that the subject of change is a river or a piece of wax, the changes open to a human mind (body) are different from those open to an angelic or divine mind or those for a dog or tree body. Second, further restrictions are induced by the particular human being whose mind (body) is under discussion. As it is with, say, rivers—the changes in geological time open to the Nile are not those open to the Amazon—it is for the human mind and body: different human minds (bodies), different change potentials.

We may summarize what the integrative framework says about the human mind in six principles that are symmetric to those it offered for the human body:

(IDM1) *Ontological primality*. The human being, for example, RD, is the entity in terms of which it is specified what DM is, that is, the mind of a man. Consequently, the conditions of DM's (i) existence and (ii) identity are specified in terms of the man whose mind it is.
(IDM2) *Essence*. DM is assigned a full-blooded essence: It is the mind of a human being.
(IDM3) *Existence*. DM existentially depends on RD (and vice versa).
(IDM4) *Endurance*. DM is a historical subject, enduring through change.

(IDM5)   *Substance.* DM is a substance in the categorical sense—a subject of a category of predications that does not itself inhere as a property in a subject.
(IDM6)   *Real distinction.* DM is really distinct, in the categorical sense if not the existential, from RD.[16]

---

16. As noted in the preface, integrative dualism excludes the coherence of the immortality of the soul. This is not a "surprise" but part and parcel of the view, just as separatist dualism makes room for the "coherence" (if not possibility) of such survival. I do not wish to engage the question of how essential was the immortality thesis to Descartes and whether he really believed in it. I think it is more illuminating to explain what framework of his allows it and what framework excludes it.

THREE

The Real Man

3.1. The Real Distinction Reviewed

By attending to their different essences, integrative dualism proves DM and DB to be numerically distinct. This preserves one of our four major assumptions—(iv) whatness separability—but with a twist because we keep the letter of the assumption but change its spirit. For now, the essence of each of the two subjects is not generic. What DM is is the mind of a man; what DB is is the body of a man. Thus DM and DB differ in their essential properties. Subjects that differ over properties are two distinct subjects. We conclude that DM and DB are *numerically* distinct. However, are they really distinct? This leads to the remaining three assumptions.

DM and DB: Complete Subjecthood and Existence Apart

Whether DM and DB are really distinct depends on our understanding of the notion of substance, or complete subject. Suppose we fix on the existential sense of complete subject: A complete subject (substance) is one that can exist all by itself. Thus an existential real distinction between purported subjects *A* and *B* demands that at least one of them can exist without the other. In this existential interpretation, integrative dualism denies complete subjecthood to RD, DM, and DB. In turn, the pair DM and DB (as well as DM-RD and DB-RD) are not existentially really distinct.

On the other hand, let us assume now the categorical conception of substance: Genuine subjecthood, in the domain of human beings but also with everything else, lies not in isolated existence but in the isolation of subjects of predication. This conception proposes that many real subjects are by their very nature existentially interdependent. This kind of interdependence is not read merely in the "weak" modal sense: Of necessity, subjects A and B coexist. Rather, a "strong" sense of dependence is contemplated here: By their very *nature* (what each is), subjects A and B coexist.

We have turned here the existential conception of real subjects on its head. Total existential independence from all others is not a mark of being real but rather of being essentially unlike the reals of the world. A real subject is embedded in the nexus of reals. And to be so embedded is to depend in the strictest way on others in the nexus. Depending on what kind of thing one is, one existentially depends on different kinds of items. So, real subjects are existentially not immaculate but are real subjects nonetheless: They are not properties or traits that describe subjects or ways of being of subjects; they are the subjects—the beings—proper. It is only in this categorical sense of "complete subject" and "real distinction" that integrative dualism preserves our assumption (i)—complete subjecthood of DM and DB.

There may be a place in the objections and replies to the Meditations where something very close to our conclusion is being debated, that is, the feasibility of nature separability without (conceivable and) existential separability. I have in mind the comment Father Caterus makes on Descartes's mind-body proof at the end of the first objections (CSM II, 72–73). Caterus points out that Scotus conceived of a form of distinction—and called it a formal distinction—in which we have "two formal concepts that are distinct prior to any operation of the intellect." God's mercy and justice may be a case in point. Nonetheless, says Caterus, "It does not follow that because justice and mercy can be conceived apart from one another they can therefore exist apart" (CSM II, 72–73).

Descartes replies that this kind of a distinction is a modal one (CSM II, 85–86). He reserves the relation to nonsubstances, specifically, to "modes," or what he also calls "incomplete entities." For this kind of entity, a modal distinction arises when we conceive of the entity by "abstraction of the intellect." It is then possible to conceive of God's justice without his mercy and vice versa; also conceivable apart are the shape and motion properties ("modes") of a thing. But, asserts Descartes, these "entities" are incomplete; they cannot exist in their own right because there is no complete understanding of the shape (motion) without the thing whose shape (motion) it is or of justice and mercy without the person who is just and merciful. From this, Descartes argues as follows: Because of this existential dependence, "I cannot imagine there to be motion in something which is incapable of shape or shape in something which is incapable of motion" (CSM II, 86). And, concludes Descartes, the mind-body conceivable separability is very different indeed: Here we do have "complete entities" and no modes. And here the conceivability apart is indicative of a genuine existential separability.

The Descartes of this reply is the existential separatist. The point Caterus is (almost) making supports our integrative dualist Descartes.

The question is how to connect (i) nature separability, (ii) conceivable separability ("in the understanding"), and (iii) existential separability. According to Descartes, we may have conceivable separability without existential separability only for incomplete entities ("abstractions") or modes. In the case of complete entities, conceivable separability reflects the availability of existential separability.

Let us grant Descartes quite a bit. First, there can be no existence and understanding of a shape (or motion) without that of which it is a shape (or motion). Let it also be granted that without existential separability, there can be no conceivable separability. This is still not enough to force on us that there can be no nature separability without conceivable and existential separability.

It may well be the case that two candidate items—each as complete a subject as could be—cannot exist apart; each exists as a subject of predication and with its own nature. I suspect that Caterus and Scotus may have realized this. What Caterus literally says (CSM II, 72–73) could run either way. He may simply say that we can conceive apart the existentially inseparable. If so, his point does not anticipate the thesis of integrative dualism-nature separability without existential and conceivable separability.

But something in his sentences—(i) "The formal concepts are distinct prior to any operation of the intellect" and (ii) "Justice and mercy *can be conceived apart of one another*"—suggests to me another reading. Regarding (i), Descartes's rheotorical slide notwithstanding, it is quite clear the "formal concepts" in question are not taken by Caterus to be incomplete entities or "intellectual abstractions." Regarding (ii), we must take notice of a slippery ambiguity in the locution "conceived apart of one another." In the first, *existential* reading, this means that x and y can be conceived to exist without each other. This is the way in which Descartes reads the locution. But we may understand it in the *existence-free numerical* reading—x and y can be conceived as two separate entities, each a distinct entity, whether or not they can be conceived to exist without each other. To my ear, the previous sentence—"Formal concepts are distinct ..."—makes the existence-free conceiving-as-an-entity-apart (though dependent on others) more plausible.

We also need not accept Descartes's view (or even its remote Aristotelian ancestry) that the existential dependence of shape, motion, justice, and mercy makes them less real beings or mere modes. We just saw that inside the lifetime metaphysics framework, the mark of being real is existential dependence on other reals. We may very well think (I do) that mind and body, too, taken as genera, or human mind and human body, as kinds, are existentially dependent on the existence of specific (human) minds and bodies. In any event, if we think that existential dependence makes the candidate a nonsubstance, we invoke an independent thesis, one separate from the particular issue I am after here: Could we have two real items whose natures are separate yet are neither existentially nor conceivably separable?

In one reading of Caterus and Scotus, I see recognition of this possibility: Prior to any intellectual operation, in rerum natura, we have formal nature separation of x and y. Thus x and y can be conceived apart from each other, as distinct entities. Yet, in no existential locus respectful of these formal natures may x be present without y and vice versa. In consequence, if our conceiving is to describe such an existential separation and it is to be respectful of the natures of x and y, it would fail.

DM and DB: Conceivable Separability

Of the four assumptions of chapter 1, three are preserved—complete subjecthood, modal indiscernability, and whatness separability. We come now to the most delicate of the four, the assumption that DM can be conceived to exist without DB.

The discussion of integrative dualism raises three separate questions about conceivability. There is, first, the question of *conceivability of disembodiment*: May DM be conceived to exist without any body—in particular DB—on hand? There are, next, two questions related to the "one man, one mind" and "one mind, one man" principles. The questions are often lumped into one in the popular personal identity discussions, where "mind-swapping" (or "body-swapping") cases are imagined as a matter of course. But there are really two separate questions to be asked. One concerns *the conceivability of mind migration*: May we conceive of this single mind, DM, that it migrates from being the mind of one man, RD, to being the mind of another man? The complementary question concerns *the conceivability of mind replacement*: May we conceive of this single man, RD, as having initially one mind, DM, then having it replaced by another mind?¹

The integrative dualism (one-one) principle does not settle the last two questions. The (one-one) principle is conceivability-free. It regards the *existence* of the items proper. It asserts that a single man has only one mind throughout its lifetime; furthermore, a single mind is throughout its lifetime the mind of one man only. This statement concerns what befalls these objects during their lifetime. It does not settle the question of what we may conceive about them.

Of course, with the help of some extra principles, we may get a quick answer to the conceivability queries. For example, suppose it were not just true or even necessarily true but in the very nature of DM to be the mind of one man only and the very essence of RD to have one fixed mind; suppose also that we agreed that whatever is flouting whatness principles is inconceivable. We would then have answers to the above conceivability questions.

But we have not yet explicitly asserted all these principles jointly. And even if we implicitly did, there remain the prima facie contrary conceivability intuitions to deal with, an intricate matter to which we now turn.

Conceivability Illusions I: Disembodiment

One of the marks of the shift from separatist to integrative dualism is the reversal of the relationship between conceivability intuitions and whatness facts. Separatist dualism starts with conceivability intuitions. It then struggles to make the relevant whatness (essence) claims respect the initial conceivability intuitions. But in the mind and heart of a separatist dualist, the

1. In the posing of these questions, the standard literature assumes that the person in question, Descartes, is not to confused with the man, the human being. When I speak of mind migration and replacement, I allude to the man Descartes.

conceivability intuition is the most basic fact, which all others must be made to respect.

Integrative dualism reverses this procedure. We do not start with our concepts and conceptual apparatus for *conceiving* mind and body. We start with the objects out there and primarily with the man, René Descartes; in turn, we continue with *his* mind and body, two subordinated objects, and no concepts whatsoever. The logic of investigation has now been reversed: The facts about what each of the trio—man, mind, and body—is are given directly, prior to, and independently of conceivability experiments. This, indeed, is the point our discussion has reached. We first analyzed, following the integrative blueprints laid out in the Mesland letter, the whatness of the mind and body of the man RD. We now face the *subsequent* question of what may be conceived of each.

Now that this is the order of investigation, a new possibility looms, *illusions of conceivability*. Typically, in such an illusion case, we *seem* to conceive of a given subject that it is a certain way. But upon consulting what this subject is, it turns out that we have not—we could not have—*really* conceived of this subject that it is this way because its being this way flouts what this subject is. So, our conceiving has never really latched on to *this* subject. We had conceived of some other subject and were taken by the illusion that we had successfully conceived of this original one. Illusions are to be expected: With the whatness of subjects given prior to our conceivings, "conceiving" has become a "success verb." There is now an independent basis for checking whether we merely seemed to have conceived a certain specific item or have really succeeded in doing so.

This standpoint provides an interesting explanation of at least one conceivability illusion of chapter 1, one had by many separatist dualists and thus by all of us at first blush: the conceivability of disembodiment. Almost everybody in my classes assents to the conceivability of DM without DB. The question is, how does this illusion arise?

The explanation I suggest is this: What we really conceive is the existence of *a* thinking being (note the italicized indefinite article) without any extended object in the story; or, we conceive of *an* extended object without any thinker around. What we go on to do is to misdescribe this successful conceiving. We declare that we have managed to conceive of a *specific* thinking subject, DM, that it exists without extended objects around. And we feel that this is an adequate description because the concept under which we carry the conceivability experiment is taken to be the full essence of the purported subject; that is, "thinking being" is the full essence of DM. If our conception respected in the story the full essence of DM, what else could disqualify the experiment?

Nothing, really, but we must be careful to latch on to the full essence of DM, not just to a thin, abstractionist-generic segment of it. Suppose now that the essence of DM is the robust property "is the mind of a human being." We can still hold on to the general principle; what we conceive while respecting DM's full essence shows us something about what can befall it. But now it is excluded by DM's very nature, that it exists without being the mind of an existing human being. Given our assumptions about the existence conditions of a human being, it is simply no longer conceivable of DM—while respecting its full essence—that it exists disembodied.

The form of explanation—including the defusing mechanism that explains the illusion of conceivability—followed here may remind the reader of the one we discussed at the end of chapter 1, in the appendix dedicated to Saul Kripke's work. Of course, Kripke is focused on the connection to real possibility and necessity, whereas we have focused on the weaker link to mere consistency with what the subject is. Nonetheless, structurally, the similarity is striking. One point is especially central—usually, we start, looking for mentally accessible *evidence*, with conceivability intuitions. We try to *find out* facts about the object's essence (possibility). Such is the order of evidence gathering—from conceivability to possibility. But things run in a reverse order when it comes to the metaphysical issue of unfolding *what makes* the pertinent facts obtain. For example, when we say that it is not possible for this table to be made of ice, what makes this fact hold has nothing to do with conceivability about this table. What is the basis for our modal fact is conceivability-free and given directly in terms of why this kind of property (wooden) but not that one (being brown) is necessary. So here we see that facts of possibility (for that matter, what the thing is) precede facts about what is genuinely conceivable. It is exactly this switch concerning the precedence of whatness to conceivability that integrative dualism performs vis-à-vis the methodology of separatist dualism.[2]

Conceivability Illusions II: Man-Mind Swaps

The preceding discussion rules out the conceivability of disembodiment by upholding two ideas. First, the projection principle—whatever is conceivable is whatness-consistent—but now read contrapositively: Whatever is whatness—inconsistent is in-

---

2. Lurking here in the background is a question that goes beyond our understanding of Descartes and concerns the metaphysics of essence and necessity per se: What may serve as conceivability-free grounds for projecting some properties as whatness pertaining and as necessary? I speculate about this (and about Kripke's ideas) in "The What and the How II," *Nous*, 1996, and "Nothing, Something, Infinity," *Journal of Philosophy*, September 1999. Further developments regarding what-x-is, e.g. is the whatness induced by the generative process that brought x into being, are pursued in "The What and The How III," in press. But see also the discussion in the following pages. In a different framework, a related departure from conceivability as the basis of (telescope into) necessity and essence is contemplated by Tom Nagel and Torin Alter op cit. ch. 1. Although our discussion is restricted to Descartes, both Nagel and Alter discuss a variety of modern claims in the philosophy of mind based on the use of conceivability exercises (e.g. the possibility of zombies and the possibility of sheer electric circuitry in a "computer" that induces consciousness). I sympathize with their discomfort with many such alleged possibilities but will not engage here in these contemporary controversies.

conceivable. Second, we insist that what DM is is the mind of a human being. Given that such a mind cannot exist without a human whose mind it is and the latter cannot exist without a body, DM cannot, in any sense, exist disembodied.

This is still consistent with conceiving this mind, DM, as the mind of another human being, say, Elizabeth, and thus as connected to another body, Elizabeth's body (EB). Such mind migration stories are familiar to us from the literature on personal identity. Also consistent so far is the conceiving of this man, RD, as shedding away his current mind, DM, and adopting a new mind, say, Elizabeth's. To exist, a man needs a man's mind, but it does not have to be his original mind.

Now, when I speak of the "consistency" of such stories, I do not mean that they represent real possibilities for the subjects concerned—RD, DM, and DB. Integral to the integrative dualism discussed above is the (one-one) principle. It guarantees that throughout the lifetime of these subjects and in whatever counterfactual possibility open to them, they are bound to each other. Nonetheless, it is consistent with what DM is—with its sheer nature—that it would be the mind of another human being ("human animal" would say the supporters of the view, just to drive the point home). And it is consistent with the nature of this man, Descartes, that he would have another mind.

As mentioned, these whatness-consistent stories are the basis for the conceivability claims of personal identity theories, which actually assert the yet stronger claim of the real possibility of such swaps. But this may be due to a general lack of distinction in this literature between a real possibility for x and a mere consistent story about x. With the distinction noted, we may reread the familiar stories as asserting the weaker claim of whatness-consistent scenarios.

What is proposed by such swap stories varies. For some writers, it is consistent with what the human being RD (not to be confused, they would say, with the *person RD*) is that the man would have another mind. For almost everyone who is friendly to such swap stories, it is obvious that it is consistent with what DM that it would be lodged in another human body and, for that matter, another human being.

The view just outlined is certainly appealing. Among many critics of classical separate dualism, the view just expounded is a natural balance point. They admit that to assert the conceivability of full disembodiment is a mistake. But equally mistaken is the attempt to deny our ability to conceive of DM without this particular body, DB, and this particular human, RD, or to deny our ability to conceive of this human being without this very specific mind, DM. I call this form of integrative dualism *generic integrative dualism* because it assigns to DM and DB the still somewhat generic essence—the mind (body) of *a* human being, of some human or other.[3]

Generic vs. Tight Integration

Descartes's texts do not contain enough information to decide the following question: Assuming that we read Descartes according to integrative lines, would he have opted for the generic form of the doctrine or a yet to be expounded, tighter variant? Rather than argue that one of these views is Descartes's own, I will discuss both forms of integration.

According to the tighter form of integration, it is not really conceivable of this mind, Descartes's, that it exists and serves as the mind of any other man. Nor is it conceivable of this man that he has any other than his actual mind and body. And this much is inconceivable *because* what DM is is not just the mind of a human being—any old one—but also the mind of this human being, René Descartes. What is asserted here in effect is

---

3. I focus here and below on a certain variant of the personal identity literature, one that insists that DM has to exist in a *human* being and body. Other variants would see any such attachment to this specific biological species of beings and their bodies as overrestrictive. The problems pointed out below in the more plausible variant apply of course to the more liberal stories.

that the force of the one-one principle of integrative dualism is not that of mere necessity; rather, it pertains to the very nature of the human mind and man whose mind it is. I call this strict version of integrative dualism *tight integrative dualism* because of the maximally specific whatnesses it assigns. What DM is is the mind of this human being, René Descartes.

Two theses proposed by this maximally specific integration call for some explanation. First, we seem to be saying that DM and EM (Elizabeth's mind) do not share whatness. This runs against the strong intuition that both are the same kind of thing, a human mind. The second point concerns conceivability issues. Familiar man-mind swapping stories (e.g., the prince-cobbler swap) suggest that mind relocation and mind replacement are coherent. It is my belief that both denials are no embarrassments but insights offered by the tighter form of integrative dualism. Let me support this claim.

First, concerning whatness, I do agree that DM and EM are the same kind of thing, a human mind. In familiar cases, this coheres with the claim that the objects share whatness. To ask of an ordinary individual like Fido, "What is Fido?" leads to the same answer as when we ask, "What kind of thing is Fido?" But when it comes to the "derivative" (as contrasted with the man Descartes) *of items*, for example, the mind and body *of* Descartes, whatness and kind questions drift apart.

Before I justify the point for DM and DB, let us consider a case from outside the mind-body realm. Consider two sets: singleton Descartes, {Descartes} and singleton Elizabeth, {Elizabeth}. Now, asked to say what is {Elizabeth}, I would answer with the set whose sole member is Princess Elizabeth; and I would give the corresponding but different answer for "What is {Descartes}?": the set whose sole member is the René Descartes. But now, asked to say what kind of thing {Elizabeth} is, I would say: a set, indeed, a singleton set. I would give the very same answer for {Descartes}. We get sameness of kind but different whatnesses.

The reason seems to me to be this: {Elizabeth} is not as "primal" an individual as Elizabeth is. To specify what the set is, we depend essentially on the more primal individual, the member of the set. The kind of thing that all singleton sets are is the same, that is, singleton sets. This classifies them all by looking for a superordinate level—their kind. And this would be the whole story were each such singleton a primal item, not one whose own whatness and identity are specified in terms of a more primal item. Thus, for Elizabeth or Fido or the Loire, all there is to the whatness is the "upward"-looking kind classification. There simply is no further "downward" specification to be made in terms of more basic individuals. But for the singleton sets of all these individuals—{Elizabeth} and others—the situation changes. There is the common upward explanation in terms of the category they belong to—their kind—but there is also the downward explanation, different for each, in terms of the individuals they are the set *of*.[4]

What is good for {Elizabeth} is good for her mind and body. The items in question are given their whatness in downward terms that relate to the man *of* whom they are the mind and body. For the superordinate kind classification, DM and EM belong in the same kind. But the downward explanation runs differently because, being of items, they are of distinct primal subjects, Descartes and Elizabeth.

In sum, the view proposed here preserves the intuition that DM and EM are the same kind of thing, a human mind, that is, the mind of a human being. But asked to say what DM is and what EM is, I find that we understate things if we do not bring out the fact that DM is the mind of this human, whereas EM is the mind of this other human. Given that this of-ness is

---

4. Of course, I here assume a certain view of Elizabeth, Fido, and the Loire. Some may wish to contest the view. For example, suppose we view the princess as derivative, say, "the union of EM and EB." In such a view, her whatness and Descartes's whatness *would* indeed differ.

essential to the very kind of thing both DM and EM are, it should come out in the specification of what each is.

Conceiving of this Specific Human Mind

I turn now to our second worry—the seemingly obvious conceivability of man-mind swaps. It is common currency in the literature on "personal identity" to *start* with conceivability experiments as ground zero of metaphysical investigations. The methodology may well be called "neo-Humean" after the practice of David Hume, even if it is another empiricist, John Locke, who inspires the ultimate views on the specific matter of personal identity. The guiding idea is that any tale that does not run into logical or otherwise a priori contradiction (among "ideas" or "concepts") is ascertained as "genuinely conceivable." In this manner, any connection between a given existing subject, for example, the Notre Dame in Paris, and any other real subject is quickly dismissed as merely contingent; in turn, any substantial property, for example, "is a cathedral," is excluded from serving as nature pertaining. In our conceiving exercises, we have subtracted any such candidates with impunity.

I thus see this general methodology as evening the score before we confront the particular case of conceivings of human minds, bodies, and beings. But even by the liberal Humean standards, it is striking how gothic the scenarios concocted in this domain are. Mind swaps are talked about as a matter of course; sometimes they are accompanied by "brain transplants," sometimes by brain "information transfers" conducted by the latest philosophical gadgets or machines; persons are easily detached from one human being (and body) and relocated in other human beings (bodies), sometimes across centuries; entire mental histories and physical makeups are transferred and reassigned by "teletransporting" devices dreamed up by Hollywood; and so on. When the shadow of doubt is expressed about the tangibility of all this metaphysical abracadabra, one is told that our inability to really carry out, in real hospitals, these transformations is a mere "technical impossibility."[5]

As mentioned, free and easy conceivability goes hand in hand with a generic essence framework. Inside this framework, the generic essence theorist seems to commit the error of separatist dualism one level higher. We gave up on the absolutely generic essence "thinking thing," but we still assign the rather generic "a human mind"; in neo-Lockean theories, we further build up a bundle of mental qualities that identify the mind. We do so by alluding to some desired stringing of memories and other cognitive faculties, making sure not to build into the bundle of mental qualities (i) the external, specific objects and kinds of which these are memories, perceptions, and so on and (ii) the human being whose memories, perceptions, and so on these are. When asked if we can conceive of this mind, DM, as existing without this man, RD, we "translate" the question to this: Can we conceive of some human mind (with, e.g., such qualitatively given memories) that it exists without this man? The answer is, yes, of course.

The response of the integrative dualist should be clear by now. It is not consistent with what DM is that it exists and the man does not. Given this, it is not really conceivable of DM—while respecting its full essence—that it exists without this man. What is conceivable is that some human mind exists without this particular man. But all of this is not conceiving of this very mind—Descartes's—as migrating to another man, actual or hypothetical.

---

5. In speaking of Hollywood films as the provider of evidence and noting a mere "technical impossibility," I quote directly from a recent series of lectures of Sidney Shoemaker at UCLA, Spring 2000. As mentioned, this line of response is common currency in the contemporary literature. I wish to note that the personal identity literature is replete with other "technology" that (i) is connected to the free and easy use of conceivability and (ii) is equally suspicious. To take a famous example, it is now standard to talk about "quasi memories," and Derek Parfit speaks of "Venetian memories," where the brain of a woman called Jane, immaculate of any contact

In the present development of the Cartesian integrative picture, all such free and easy conceivability claims are ungrounded. The original sin, the conjuring trick, is the Humean essence-obliviousness of the basic notion of seeming conceivability (imaginability). To remind us, the integrative Cartesian framework starts with essence, one founded on a robust endurance metaphysics. This means that worldly items—the stone and the sun; the river and the piece of wax; the human body, mind, and being—not only change in history but also come into and go out of existence in history. It is the process of a subject's coming into history that determines (i) *what*, for example, this thing taken from the honeycomb is and (ii) of the many wax pieces, *which* one was thus generated. Descriptions of the lifetime of the piece of wax rest on what it took to generate this life-in-time in the first place.

So far this holds of pieces of wax, and if we abide by the-wax-is-the-model principle, the same applies to the emergence of human minds. Within the neo-Humean and Lockean methodology, it is easy to conceive of DM as existing in the human being Plato a couple of millennia before it was actually generated in the man Descartes. It is also easy to imagine it just "leaping into existence," "joining" with some human body to

---

with the city of Venice, is implanted with "memory traces" from to a man called Paul and gotten by him through direct perception in the piazzas and by the canals. I see these as sheer logical constructions tagged misleadingly to suggest kinship with an existing species of phenomena. None of these familiar constructions has anything—verbal excesses aside—to do with the real, cognitive process of memory. I am not merely expressing doubt about the genuineness of the *possibility* of applying such a supposedly coherent notion of memory to beings like us. I question the very coherence of the idea as a notion of memory for any historically real, existing species and/or for human beings. I do not pursue here these grave reservations. In the text, I focus on the use of this one technology in the current literature that is (i) relatively informal and (ii) pertinent to the sustenance of separatist dualist theses.

"form" a subsequent man. But this is not so in the current integrative picture. To replay Descartes's own analogy of the arm-body relation: A human mind is engendered as part of the natural development of a human being and its human body. We might well speak of its generation process as part of the overall human morphogenesis; only when a certain stage in the emergence of the human being, specifically of his or her brain, has been reached, will a human mind come into being. The process is specific to kinds of beings; that is, an angelic mind would not emerge in the way a human mind does. The process is also specific to the very human being that is its breeding ground—this mind, DM, grew as part of the growth of this very human being, RD. The genitive form is absolutely essential here: It is this being's mind, the mind of this being.

We are now ready to go back to what is conceivable of DM as a function of what it is. It is only within this distinct being in cosmic history, René Descartes, that this mind, DM, had a way of coming into real life. It is thus only as this being's mind that it has any *conceivable* life.

3.2. The Primal Question and the Primal Answer

From the very start, Descartes's project was threatened by *the prove too little/prove too much dilemma*. It is time to evaluate how the integrative interpretation handles this threat.

The discussion of existential separability and illusions of conceivability points out that Descartes has grounds for claiming that he does not "prove too much." Integrative dualism does not separate mind and body so radically as to claim that they can exist without the other, blurring the sense that they are essentially interdependent parts of the single person each of us is.

Descartes is also in a position to claim that he escapes the "prove too little" horn. The primality of the human being is the cornerstone of the integrative interpretation; the mind and body are given as those of a human being. Nonetheless, the primality of the man does not denigrate the status of his mind and body to that of mere modes. The mind and body of the man are genuine, complete subjects, not engendered by the existential gloss of "subject." But, then, neither is the man himself an existentially independent being nor is a variety of other mundane subjects dear to Descartes—the sun, the Loire, Mt. Blanc, the piece of wax, or any other worldly item—for all depend on other real beings for their existence. And so, sticking to our categorical notion of a subject in general and in the realm of man in particular, we count all three, DM, DB, and RD, as complete subjects. They are existentially interdependent but categorically separate; each is a being, not merely a way-of-being.

Safely out of the dilemma's claws, we have left one question unattended—the primal question. We have not answered the opening question, "What am I?"

Having been exposed to integrative dualism about the man-mind-body trio, many surmise that the integrative answer is something like this: What I am is the union of a human mind and a human body. Taking this to be the answer, many suspect a "vicious circularity." We have been articulating the essence of DM and DB in terms of the human being they are the mind and body of; and now, the essence of the human being RD is given in terms of the union of DM and DB. The mind and body explained by way of the man, the man by way of the (his) mind and body.

I believe such circularity is not vicious, partly because Descartes's quest here is not for a definition (see below). But my main answer is that the proposal—what I am is the union of a human mind and body—is not the one given by the integrative picture. The answer it gives on behalf of Descartes is the one he gives originally in Meditation II, immediately after the question mark of "What am I?"—that is, "a man." I allow myself to call it not just his first answer but also "the primal answer."

In the original text of Meditation II (quoted in this book's preface) and the companion, "The Search for Truth," Descartes mentions problems in holding to this answer:

> POLYANDER: You did not want to ask anything which could not be answered very easily. So I shall say I am a *man*.
>
> EUDOXUS: You are not paying attention to my question and the reply you give, however simple it may seem to you, would plunge you into very difficult and complicated problems, were I to press you even a little. If, for example, I were to ask even Epistemon what a man is, and he gave the stock reply of the scholastics, that a man is a "rational animal" and, if, in order to explain these two terms (which are just as obscure as the former), he were to ask us further, through all the levels which are called "metaphysical", we should be dragged into a maze from which it would be impossible to escape. For two questions arise from this one. First, what is an *animal*? second, what is *rational*? if in order to explain what an animal is, he were to reply that it is a "living and sentient being," that a living being is an "animate body" and that a body is a "corporeal substance", you see immediately that the questions, like the branches of a family tree, would rapidly increase and multiply. Quite clearly the result of all these admirable questions would be pure verbiage, which would elucidate nothing and leave us in our original state of ignorance. (CSM II, 410)[7]

So runs Descartes's nightmare scenario of what might ensue if we gave the primal answer to the primal question. The passage seems to me to raise three separate issues.

---

7. Italics are in the original.

One problem concerns the purported *form*, according to Descartes, of the critical truth: To be a man is to be a rational animal. A second question concerns what, according to Descartes, is the *truth* of the matter; that is, is "rational animal" the right answer? These two questions focus on Descartes's view. A third and final question goes beyond Descartes's scholarship and enters into plain metaphysics: What are we doing when we say that "what I am is a . . . " and, in particular, when we inject in the space the common noun "man"?

I will start with the two Descartes-bound questions. Concerning the form of the purported "definition"—Man is a rational animal—Descartes is relating to a long tradition before him, a tradition that reached a high point in late medieval philosophy. And in spite of Descartes's discomfort with it, the tradition went on to dominate many philosophical discussions, for example, Kant's, all the way into our century. Roughly (and no more than a rough idea is ever given), the "logical form" of the statement is that of a "definition." This is taken to assert something displayed by "Man = $_{df}$ rational animal."

Are the relata here concepts, properties, or names of species and genera? Is the identity sign to be taken seriously? I do not know. What is more, the general presumption of such definition is that on the right-hand side we are to get a "reduction," a relatum "made up" of more basic ingredients (concepts, properties, etc.) than the one preceding the copula. This is even more confusing because an identity sign is used. In a real identity, for example, "M. Monroe = Norma Jean Baker," there is no reduction on the right-hand side, nor do we get with genuine identities complaints of circularity (arising from the expectation that we were to be offered a noncircular reduction).

I will not dwell on this medieval theory of real definition that haunted Descartes because I feel that he is absolutely right to avoid it. Let me just record, rather than argue for, two observations.

One observation is that even the theory's idealized model— whatness statements in mathematics—is mishandled. Suppose I say, "What 9 is is a number" or "What the doubleton {Elizabeth, Descartes} is is a set," and you question me: "But what is a number? What is a set?" What I give you in return is not a definition—not even an implicit definition—of "number" and "set." Perhaps some formalist philosophers of mathematics would give you such a definition. But my *explanation* of what a number is and what a set is would not be by way of a definition. And whatever form it would take, it would use related arithmetic notions of order (finitude) and set theoretic notions of collection and would thus seem to be "circular." So, even in accounting for the whatness of mathematical entities, the real definition model seems to me misguided.

Concerning the other observation, suppose we move from mathematics to such questions as "What is Fido?"—to which the right answer, intuitively speaking, must be "a dog." You now challenge me: "But what is a dog?" Most likely I would answer: "a certain kind of mammalian species"; perhaps, in a genetics laboratory, I would add: "a mammalian species of characteristic DNA D"; or in an evolutionary biology class, I would add: "a mammalian species originating in ur-group U"; and so on. Take any such answer—none is a *definition* of the species dog, the property of being a dog, the property of being a member of the species dog, and so on. My statements are all further whatness statements about any one of those, say, the species dog, just as the previous one was a whatness statement about Fido. That initial whatness statement did not define Fido. It provided a property of Fido that was essential to it, articulated what kind of thing it is, classified it by way of a fundamental biological ensemble it is a member of, and so on. None of this had the form of an identity or a reduction or replacement of poor Fido by a logical construction out of a bundle of properties or out of a genus and differentia or the like. I first said what kind of thing Fido is, then what kind of thing the species dog is. That is all.

In answering the question "What am I?" Descartes does not need to carry on his shoulders the excesses of medieval definitionalism. Perhaps there is something intrinsically elusive about the form of a statement such as "What Fido is is a dog" and "What dog is is a mammalian species." But we cannot give up in advance on such statements just because medieval definitionalists mistreated them.

So far this discussion has concerned Descartes's worries about the form of the whatness statement. My second question concerns the truth of the matter, at least from Descartes's standpoint. Parts of his work—surely his work on language as distinguishing us from animals in a most fundamental way—suggest strongly that any classification of humans as a kind of animal is just wrong. If so, the problem with the primal answer is that it leads to a statement—Man is rational animal—that is simply false.

Suppose this is Descartes's last word on the matter. Then, all that follows is that what it is to be a man—which he is and I am—is not essentially to be a kind of animal. But what I am and he is is still given by the answer: "a man." And since the answer "To be a man is to be a rational animal" has now been disqualified as false, Descartes is free to pursue his own answer about what it is to be a man. Whatever this subsequent answer is, the answer to his initial question—"What am I"?—is still "a man."

So far we assume a reading of Descartes that denies that what it is to be a man is to be a certain kind of animal. Now, for myself, I do not believe that in order to make sense of Descartes's answering with "a man" the "What am I?" query, we need to take a stand on whether he ultimately saw mankind as an animal kind. All we need to make sense of is his prime assertion—"What I am is a man"—and then of related assertions such as "What Fido is is a dog"; "What the Loire is is a river";"what Hon is is (a piece of) wax."

In addressing the third question, how to understand such whatness assertions, we need yet again to separate matters of logical form and matters of truth. The former seem to me to pose problems at a much more sophisticated level. Let me give a sense of this in order to eliminate much of the sophistication and focus on the truth of the matter.

First, form: Consider our kind-specifying assertions—"Descartes is a man," "Fido is a dog," and "The Loire is a river." The proper name refers here to a certain individual, not a property or a concept or a predicate. But what are we to say of the indefinite noun phrase that follows "is"? Are we attributing a property to the individual named by the proper name, as if we were using an adjective, as in "Descartes is wise"? Or might we still be referring, even on the right-hand side of the "is," this time to a different object, a kind—for example, mankind—and saying overall that Descartes is a member of this kind?

Such a referent for the common noun would be a bona fide historical object, whether it is a chemical substance (like wax), a geological kind (like a river), or a biological species (the way I take mankind and dogkind to be; "biological" is not to say that mankind is just another animal kind). Such historical objects are part of the cosmological order of things: They come into being at a certain point in the history of the cosmos; for example, none of the preceding kinds existed three minutes after the Big Bang, although, say, the kind hydrogen did. Such cosmological kinds go on existing in time and changing through history, losing and gaining members and becoming widespread and endangered. Eventually, they—the kinds—might go out of existence if the cosmos were to so evolve to exclude the existence of members of the kind. In this sense, mankind is no eternal platonic being but one that came to be (not, e.g., 5000 years ago but around 3 million years ago), a kind that currently exists but is subject to the danger of going out of existence. Under this understanding, in saying of Fido (Descartes) that what it is is a dog (man), we are relating two historical beings. We are saying what the specific individual (Fido) is by assigning it to certain natural ensemble (kind of things), itself existing in history and fundamental to the description of cosmological evolution.

Here, then, are two simple theories of the form of what is said in whatness-specifying assertions such as "The Loire is a river," "Descartes is a man," and "Fido is a dog." One views the form as predicative—that is, the assignment of a property, a kind property, to a real subject, something the modern logician would code by the predicative form "Fa." The other sees the form as a relation between two objects, the individual subject being said to be a member of the kind referred to by the common noun (what the logician would code by a form analogous to the set theoretic relation "Item a is a member of the set S"). Both theories are interesting, and the question of which one is right is none too easy to answer.[8]

The preceding discussion concerns sophisticated questions about the form of the whatness specifying assertion "Descartes is a man." These form-related questions are intriguing and worth pursuing in the right context. But my point here is that we need not await the verdict of these refined discussions of logical form to be in a position to *make sense* of Descartes's primal answer to his primal question. Whatever theory of form is ultimately correct, we know this much: Just as the assertion that what Fido is is a dog, the assertion that what I am is a man makes sense and needs no philosophical analysis to be seen to make sense. Moreover, just as the assertion that what Fido is is a dog, the claim that what I am is a man has the undeniable ring of truth. So does Descartes's line to Elizabeth: "Everyone feels that he is a single person with both body and thought so related by nature that the thought can move the body and feel the things which happen to it." One finds with Descartes, as with the mind-body problem in general, that illumination may lie not so much in the murkiest depths of scholastic analysis but in taking notice of limpid shallows.

---

8. In a rather different, technical context, I discussed in detail the form of such statements as "Descartes is a man" and the role of the indefinite noun phrase that follows the "is." See "The Subject-Verb-Object Class," *Philosophical Perspectives* 12 I, II (1998).

It would be enlightening to have at some point a general theory of the logical form of such what-I-am assertions. It would surely help to have a general metaphysical theory of the whatness of kinds—what are the kinds *dog*, *wax*, *river*, or *man*? In the latter case, it is very likely that mere DNA specification or the tracing of a historical connection to some ur-men in Ethiopia would not be a fully satisfying answer, at least not for someone with a Cartesian bent. We are likely to call on the observation that each man has a mind and body; that they are interdependent (perhaps in the way discussed above); that they are essentially and distinctively a human (mankind) mind and body; that there is no understanding of being of that kind— being a man—without a better understanding of how each such being depends on the existence of his mind and body.

All of these metaphysical extras would help. But whatever appeal such theoretical analyses might have and whatever confidence we may come to have in them, they are not likely to exceed the appeal and confidence we find in Descartes's primal answer to the primal question.

Index

a priori knowledge, conceivability and, 19, 21, 48
abstraction
  in real distinction, 101
  of whatness, 30–31, 33
abstractionist metaphysics
  of human mind, 91–93
  lifetime theories *versus*, 84–86, 96–97
  of numerical sameness, 82–83, 86
  of objects, 84, 86, 88–89
allusion, in mentality, 54
analog, in pain distinction, 45
angelic mind
  in integrative dualism, 79
  in separatist dualism, 62–63
  stability of, 94–95
animal, rational, man as, 117–123
arm-body connection, 67nn.2,3, 73, 90, 95n.14, 115
Arnauld
  on conceivability, 16, 18, 20–23, 42–43
  on possibility, 15n.5, 16–20, 23
  on real distinction, 12n.3, 13n.4
  on whatness, 23–42

atoms, 88
attributes, in separatist dualism, 62–63, 67–68

being, of substance, 69
bodies
  composition of, 81, 81n.9
  Descartes's cuts for, 75–76, 76n.7, 81
  endurance in time of, 74–75, 77, 87
  of a given kind, 76–79
  human (*see* human body)
body-in-general, separatist conception of, 74–75, 80
body-swapping, 78n.8, 96n.15, 103. *See also* mind-swapping
brain, as mind model, 91, 95n.14
brain state, of pain, mental state *versus*, 44–48
brain transplants, 112, 113n.5

C fibers. *See* firing of C fibers
can, in real distinction, 4, 6, 8, 12
can exist without the other, in real distinction, 4, 6

Cartesian concepts, 8, 59, 114
  of subjects in time, 81–98
categorical conception
  of real subjects, 70
  of substance, 67–68, 77, 100
categorical real distinction, 70
change. *See also* transformation
  human mind endurance of, 90–93, 97
  robust whatness and, 87–88, 90, 93, 93n.12
coevolution, of humans, 85, 121
cognition. *See* thinking
coherent separation, of possibility, 13, 13n.4, 15
coherent story
  in real distinction, 8–10, 12–13, 12n.3
  in whatness quest, 8–10, 38–39, 98n.16
coherent story projection, 12
combinatorialist view, of possibility, 14
complete idea
  framework for understanding, 31–33
  in whatness, 22–23, 29–33
complete subjecthood
  denial of, 99–100
  existence apart and, 99–103
  in integrative dualism, 59, 61, 66, 70
complete thing
  existence-free terms for, 67–69, 69n.4
  notion of, 31–33, 66
  in separatist dualism, 66–68, 67n.2

completeness, notion of, 31–33, 66
conarion hypothesis, of mind-body connection, 91
conceivability
  Arnauld's notion of, 16, 18, 20–23, 42–43
  autonomy of, 42–43
  constraining of, 25–26, 29
  de re notions of, 93n.12
  Descartes's notion of, 16, 30–31, 42–44
  determinism of, 20
  of idea, 22–23
  illusions of, 105, 115
  imaginability *versus*, 52n.15, 53–54, 56, 58, 114
  integrative dualism and, 103–105, 107–108
  of life, 115
  logical, 43–48
  of mathematics, 14, 17, 19, 23
  metaphysical, 10–11, 42–43, 107
  of mind migration, 103
  possibility as preceding, 107
  primacy of, 20–23, 30
  a priori knowledge in, 19, 21, 48
  projection method for, 10–13, 11n.2, 13n.4, 18
  in real distinction, 5–6, 10–11, 59, 101, 103–104
  of reality, 21–23
  seeming *versus* real, 19, 62, 66n.1
conceivability illusions
  disembodiment as, 23n.7, 103–107, 109

extendedness in, 106
man-mind swaps as, 103–104, 107–109
conceivability intuitions, 57, 104–106, 111
evidence in, 106–107, 111
whatness facts and, 104–107
conceivability-reflecting-reality projection principle, 21–22
conceivable separability, 59, 101, 103–104
conceivably-exists-without-the pertinent-physicalium, 43
conceivably so and so, 46–47
conceptual fix
application of, 25, 41
constraints in, 25–26, 29
epistemic fact of, 27–28
metaphysical fact of, 27–29
theoretical basis of, 23n.7, 24
consistency
in man-mind swaps, 107–108
possibility *versus*, 37
consistent-with-what-it-is-to-not-be-extended, 38
constraints, in conceptual fix theory, 25–26, 29
corpse, as thing, 78
creation point, of subject, 32–33, 33n.12

data articulation, of projection mold, 11
de dicto argument
epistemological gains of, 48–49, 52
for mind-body connection, 45–48

de re argument
for cognition, 56, 56n.18
for mind-body connection, 44–47
premise of, 48–49, 53
definition, in primal answer, 118–120
dependence
existential, 102–103
in real distinction, 52n.15, 56
derepresentation, in de dicto premise, 49
derivatives, in integrative dualism, 110–111
Descartes, René
on conceivability, 16, 30–31, 42–44
cuts of generic bodies, 75–76, 76n.7, 81
on imagination, 56
letter to Mesland, 71–72, 72n.5, 76, 79–81, 95
meditations of (*see* specific meditation)
on pain and brain states, 44, 47
on possibility, 14–16, 15n.5, 23
on primal question, 115–123
on whatness, 23–25, 28–29, 38–42
desires, in real distinction, 81n.9
determinism, of conceivability, 20
disembodiment
in integrative dualism, 60, 103–107, 109
in real distinction, 19, 23n.7, 25

INDEX

distinction
  of individuals, 5
  in real distinction, 12–13, 12n.3, 100
distinctness of discernibles
  applications of, 5–8, 13n.4
  Cartesian doubt of, 8
divine mind
  in separatist dualism, 62–63
  stability of, 94
dual key project, objectives of, xvii
dualism
  forms of, xviii
  integrative (*see* integrative dualism)
  metaphysical, 62, 65, 74, 77, 78n.8
  numerical sameness in, 70, 73
  separatist (*see* separatist dualism)

endurance
  of mind-body connection, 63–66, 71–81, 85–93
  of piece-of-wax-as-a model, 85–89
  of subjects in time, 65–66, 85–91
endurance in time
  abstractionist theory of, 83
  of bodies
    generic, 74–75, 87
    given kind, 77
  of minds
    generic, 79–81, 97
    human, 71–72, 79
  of objects, 74–76, 86–87
  of subjects, 65–66, 85–91

epistemic conceivability
  metaphysical *versus*, 42–43
  of pain, 43, 48–49, 52
  preservation of, 39
  transparency of, 18–21, 43, 48–49
epistemic possibility, in real distinction, 4, 8
epistemic whatness
  evaluation of, 38–41
  notion of, 24–27
essence
  abstractionist theory of, 83
  of bodies
    generic, 4, 75
    given king, 77
  generic, 62–64, 71, 75, 109–112
  metaphysics of, 170n.2
  of mind, 80, 90–91, 97
  of real pain, 52, 54
  robustness of, 87–88, 90, 93, 93n.12
  of separability, 62–64, 75
  of whatness, 5, 52, 54, 64–65, 104
essentialism, 38
Euclidean axioms, 37
evaluation worlds, in de dicto premise, 49
evidence
  in conceivability intuitions, 106–107, 111
  of specific human mind, 112–113, 113n.5
exclusion
  necessity *versus*, 33–34
  in whatness, 8–10, 30–33, 39

existence
  of bodies
    generic, 75
    given kind, 77–79
  of mind, 80, 97
  necessary connections and, 52n.15
  in real distinction, 4, 25, 39, 60, 99–103, 106
existence apart, complete subjecthood and, 99–103
existence-free numerical reading, of distinct entities, 102
existence in time. *See* endurance in time
existential conception, of substance, 67
existential dependence, 102–103
existential independence, 68, 70, 75, 79, 100
existential real distinction, 5–8, 70, 101, 115
existential sameness, numerical, 102
existential separability
  of mind and body, 61–62, 66, 81n.9, 115
  of real distinction, 5–8, 70, 101
experiences
  as phenomenon, 56–58
  predication of, 55
extended thing, 38, 88–89, 106
extendedness
  in conceivability illusions, 106
  of human body, 62, 65, 82
  of whatness, 9, 15, 17, 38, 89
extension to mind, Kripke's notion of, 54–55
external, as what it seems, 52, 92

f mind, separatist conception of, 80–81
fictional characters, creation of, 33, 33n.12
finite sets, in mathematics, 35–36, 36n.13, 119
firing of C fibers (FCF)
  mental state *versus* brain state of, 44–48
  pain *versus*, 44, 52, 52n.15
formal distinction, in complete subjecthood, 100–101

generic bodies, Descartes's cuts of, 75–76, 76n.7, 81
generic essence theory
  of integrative dualism, 71, 74–76, 109–112
  of separatist dualism, 62–64, 75
geometry
  disanalogy with mind-body connection, 23–24, 26
  in real distinction, 14, 17, 19
  as whatness example, 27–28, 34, 37
God
  justice of, 100–102
  mercy of, 100–102

histories
  of different minds, 63, 65
  of subjects, 81, 83
human being
  modes of, 60–61, 116
  as particular, 86, 89, 109, 109n.3, 113
  primal answer of, 116–123
  primal question of, 115–116

human being (*continued*)
    primality of, xviii, 60–61, 66, 71, 76–80, 96–97, 111
    prove too much/prove too little dilemma of, 59–61, 115–123
    as rational animal, 117–123
human body
    connection to mind (*see* mind-body connection)
    endurance of, 63–66, 74–77, 85, 87–88, 90–91
    existential separation of, 5, 61–62, 66, 81n.9
    extendedness of, 62, 65, 82
    integrative dualism of, 72–79
    whatness of, 77–78, 78n.8
human involvement, freedom from, 71
human mind
    abstractionist metaphysics of, 91–93
    connection to body (*see* mind-body connection)
    endurance of, 63–66, 71–72, 79–81, 85, 90–93, 97
    existential separation of, 5, 61–62, 66, 81n.9
    generic essence of, 62–64, 71, 75, 109–112
    integrative dualism of, 72–74, 79–81
    intellectual qualities of, 38, 81–82, 81n.9, 91
    mental categories of, 56–58
    momentary, 92
    nature of, 81–82, 81n.9, 91, 96
    one-one principle of, 94–96, 95n.14
    prime lifetime fact of, 93–94
    as specific, 112–115, 113n.5
Hume, David, on personal identity, 112–114

idea
    complete (*see* complete idea)
    conceivability of, 22–23
    of substance, 3
identity
    criteria for, 45
    in pain distinction, 45
    personal, 64, 66n.1, 95, 96n.15, 108, 109n.3
    in primal answer, 118–119
    in real distinction, 12, 12n.3
    specific man-mind swaps and, 112–114, 113n.5
illusions of conceivability, 105, 115
imaginability. *See also* perceptual states
    conceivability *versus*, 52n.15, 53–54, 56, 58, 114
    Kripke's notion of, 52n.15, 53–54, 56
    mental *versus* sensational, 55–58
    predication in, 53–54
    seeming *versus* real, 49–51, 52n.15, 53, 58
imagination, in de dicto premise, 49
immortality, of soul, 98n.16
incomplete idea, notion of, 32
independence
    existential, 68, 70, 75, 79, 100
    of mind and body, 62–63, 66, 96n.15
    symmetrical, 62–63

individuals, transformation of, 89
infinite sets, in mathematics, 35–36, 36n.13
information transfer, 91, 112
inseparability, modal, 59–61
integrative dualism, 71–81
  of bodies, 72–74
    generic, 74–76
    given kind, 76–79
  complete subjecthood in, 59, 61, 66, 70
  denial of, 99–100
  conceivability and, 103–105, 107–108
  derivatives in, 110–111
  disembodiment illusion in, 60, 103–107, 109
  generic, 71, 74–76, 109–112
  of human mind, 72–74, 79–81
  Meditation II on, 71, 74, 76, 79–81
  Mesland letter on, 71–72, 72n.5, 76, 79–81, 95
  of mind-body connection, xvii–xviii, 39, 72–81
  of-ness principle in, 111–112
  of primality of man, 111, 115–116
  principles of, 78n.8, 96–98
  separatist dualism *versus*, 61, 71, 96n.15
  set theory of, 110–111
  symmetrical, 71–74, 80, 94n.13, 97
  tight, 109–112
intellectual abstraction, of whatness, 30–31, 33

intellectualism
  of human mind, 38, 81–82, 81n.9, 91
  perceptual states and, 56
intentional action states, as phenomenon, 56–58
interdependence, of subjects, 79
internal, as what it feels like, 92
intuitions
  about identity of thoughts, 57, 104
  conceivability, 57, 104–106, 111
items. *See* object(s); subject(s)

justice
  apart from mercy, 102
  of God, 100–101

kind-blind attributes, in separatist dualism, 62–63
kind-specifying assertions, in primal answer, 120–123
knowledge, prior. *See* a priori knowledge
Kripke, Saul
  on conceivability, 42–44
  morals of, 53–54
  on pain phenomenon, 44, 52, 52n.15, 54–55, 55n.16, 57
  on real possibility-imaginability, 49–51

language theory, in pain distinction, 45–46
life, coevolution of, 85, 121
lifetime metaphysics, of enduring objects, 84–86

lifetime principles
  abstractionists *versus*, 83, 96–97
  of subjects in time, 65–66, 93–98
limits, in set theory, 35
living, coevolution of, 85, 121
Locke, John
  on personal identity, 112–114
  on whatness, 9
logic, modal. *See* modal logic
logical conceivability, metaphysical *versus* epistemologic argument for, 43–48
logical possibility
  in real distinction, 4, 11–12, 12n.3
  in whatness evaluation, 38–39, 123
logical potential, 84

magnetic resonance imaging (MRI), of pain distinction, 44–47
man. *See* human being
man-mind-body trio, 116
man-mind swaps. *See* body-swapping; mind-swapping
man relocation, integration with, 110
materiality, of whatness, 9
mathematics
  conceivability of, 14, 17, 19, 23
  in dualism theories, 70, 73
  set theory of, 34–36, 36n.13, 119
  whatness of, 27–28, 34–35, 118–119

matter, particles of, 81–82, 82n.9, 88
Meditation II
  on integrative dualism, 71, 74, 76, 79–81
  on primal question, 116–117
  on real distinction, 8–10, 28–29, 38
  on separatist dualism, 62–63, 65
  on subjects in time, 82–83, 90
Meditation III, on real distinction, 22, 28
Meditation VI, on real distinction, 4, 28, 90–91
memory implants, 112, 113n.5
mental categories, of human mind, 56–58
mental items
  conceivings of, 43
  imaginability of, 54–55
mental state
  of pain
    brain state *versus*, 44–48
    extension to, 54–55, 55n.16
    predication and, 54–55, 55n.16
mercy
  apart from justice, 102
  of God, 100–101
Mesland letter, on integrative dualism, 71–72, 72n.5, 76, 79–81, 95
metaphysical conceivability
  epistemology *versus*, 42–43
  in real distinction, 10–11, 107
metaphysical dualism
  integrative, 74, 77, 78n.8
  separatist, 62, 65

metaphysical possibility
    Kripke's notion of, 49–51
    in real distinction, 4, 15n.5
    of whatness, 24–26
metaphysical potential, 84
metaphysical whatness
    evaluation of, 38–39, 41
    factual basis of, 27–29
    of kinds, 121, 123
    possibility of, 24–26
metaphysics
    abstraction (*see* abstractionist metaphysics)
    of essence, 170n.2
    lifetime, of enduring objects, 84–86
    of necessity, 170n.2
    of subjects in time, 83–84, 86–87
    subspecies-aeternitate, 83
mind
    of angels, 62–63, 79, 94–95
    composition of, 81, 81n.9
    essence of, 80, 90–91, 97
    generic idea of, 80–81, 85
    of a god, 62–63, 94
    of humans (*see* human mind)
    lifetime principles of, 93–98
    possible histories of, 63, 65
    separatist conception of, 80–81
mind-body connection. *See also* human body; human mind
    Cartesian concept of, 8, 59
    conceivability of, 21
    de re *versus* de dicto arguments for, 43–48
    as dilemma, xvii–xviii, xviiin.1
    endurance of, 63–66, 71–77, 85–88, 90–91
    geometric disanalogy of, 23–24, 26
    integrative, 79–81
    necessity of, 39
    pineal location of, 91
    possibility of, 19–20
    primal answer to, 116–123
mind-body independence, 62–63, 66, 96n.15
mind-in-general, 80–81
mind migration, conceivability of, 103, 104n.1, 108
mind replacement
    conceivability of, 103–104, 104n.1
    integration with, 110
mind-swapping
    as conceivability illusions, 103–104, 107–109
    conceivability of, 107–109, 112
    integration of, 110
    possibility of, 103–104, 107–109
    in real distinction, 103–104, 107–109, 112, 113n.5
    specific identity and, 112–115, 113n.5
    types of, 103–104, 104n.1
    whatness-consistency in, 107–108
minds, endurance in time of
    generic, 79–81, 97
    human, 71–72, 79
modal inseparability, 59–61

134 INDEX

modal logic
    of complete subjecthood, 100–101
    failure of, 24–25, 29
    in pain phenomenon, 44, 46, 49
    of possibility, 4, 12n.3, 15, 25
    of primality of human being, 60–61
modes
    of human being, 60–61, 116
    in real distinction, 101
    of substances, 67–68
momentary mind, 92

nature, of human mind, 81–82, 81n.9, 91, 96
nature separability, 101
nature thinking, 38
necessary union hypothesis, 37
necessity
    of connections between distinct existence, 52n.15
    exclusion *versus*, 33–34
    metaphysics of, 17on.2
    in whatness, 28–29, 33–38, 40, 107n.2
no endurance theory
    of separatist dualism, 63–66
    of subject, 65–66
nothing is quite what it seems, 51–52
numerical sameness
    abstractionist theory of, 82–83, 86
    in dualism theories, 70, 73
    existential, 102

object(s)
    conceptual fix theory of, 23n.7, 24, 26
    endurance in time, 74–76, 86–87
    metaphysics of, 84–86, 88–89
    seeming *versus* real
        conceivability of, 19, 62, 66n.1
        imaginability of, 49–53, 52n.15, 58
    transformation of, 88–89
objectal relation
    in real distinction, 12, 12n.3
    in reality reflection, 22–23
    in whatness, 24, 33n.12
of-ness principle
    in integrative dualism, 111–112
    as lifetime, 94–95, 94n.13
one-one principle
    failure of, 103–104
    as lifetime, 94–96, 95n.14

pain
    essence of real, 52, 54
    firing of C fibers *versus*, 44, 52, 52n.15
    imagined, 52
    Kripke's notion of, 44, 52, 52n.15, 54–55, 55n.16, 57
    mental state *versus* brain state of, 44–48
    transparent epistemology argument for, 43, 48–49, 52
particles, of matter, 81–82, 82n.9, 88

particularism, of human being, 86, 89, 109, 109n.3, 113
perceptual states. *See also* imaginability
  intellectual states and, 56
personal identity
  man-mind swaps and, 112–115, 113n.5
  theory of, 64, 66n.1, 95, 96n.15, 108, 109n.3
phenomenon
  experiences as, 56–58
  mental states as, 56–58
  necessity in whatness as, 34
  pain distinction as, 44–45, 49, 52, 52n.15, 54–55, 55n.16, 57
physical qualities
  of bodies, 81–82, 82n.9
  transformation of, 88–89
piece-of-wax-as-a model
  endurance of, 85–89
  principles of, 85n.10, 90–91
  as subject in time, 82–85, 114–115
pineal gland, 91
plurality, in set theory, 35
possibility
  Arnauld's notion of, 15n.5, 16–20, 23
  combinatorialist view of, 14
  consistency *versus*, 37
  Descartes's notion of, 14–16, 15n.5, 23
  logical, 4, 11–12, 12n.3, 38–39, 123
  of man-mind swaps, 103–104, 107–109
  metaphysical, 4, 15n.5, 24–26, 49–51
  as preceding conceivability, 107
  primacy of, 17–20
  projection method for, 10–13, 12n.3, 13n.4, 17–18, 39
  in real distinction, 4–7, 10
possibility tout court, 15n.5
potential, 4
  of subjects in time, 84
predicates and predication
  experiential, 55
  in imaginability, 53–54
  mental, 54–55, 55n.16
  of substance, 67–68, 79, 98
primal answer
  definition in, 118–120
  to primal question, 116–123
primal question, 115–116
  primal answer to, 116–123
primality
  of bodies, 74–78
  integrative interpretation of, 111, 115–123
  of real man, xviii, 60–61, 66, 71, 76–80, 96–97, 111
prime lifetime fact, of mind, 93–94
projection mold, two-step, 11
projection principles
  conceivability-reflecting-reality, 21–22
  in man-mind swaps, 107–108
  in real distinction, 10–13, 11n.2, 13n.4, 18, 39
projection step, of projection mold, 11

prove too much/prove too little dilemma
  integrative interpretation of, 115–123
  in separatist dualism, 59–61, 66
Pythagorean theorem, 14, 17, 19
  whatness and, 28, 34

quasi-demonstrative representations, in de dicto premise, 56n.18

rational animal, man as, 117–123
real conceivability, seeming conceivability *versus*, 19, 62, 66n.1
real conceivability projection, 10–13, 11n.2, 13n.4, 18
real distinction
  Arnauld's notion of, 12n.3, 13n.4
  basis for, 3–7, 70
  of bodies
    generic, 75
    given kind, 77
  categorical, 70
  coherent stories in, 8–10, 12–13, 12n.3, 98n.16
  complete subjecthood in, 99–103
  conceivable separability in, 5–6, 10–11, 59, 101, 103–104, 107
  Descartes's meditations on, 4, 8–10, 22, 28–29, 38, 90–91
  disembodiment illusion in, 23n.7, 103–107, 109
  existence in, 4, 25, 39, 60, 106
    as apart, 99–103
  existential separability of, 5–8, 70, 101, 115
  generic *versus* tight integration of, 109–112
  man-mind swaps in, 103–104, 107–109, 112, 113n.5
  of mind, 80, 98
  necessary connections and, 52n.15
  observations of, 52n.15, 56, 101
  projection method for, 10–13, 11n.2, 13n.4, 18, 39
  simpliciter, 70
  of specific human mind, 112–115, 113n.5
real imaginability, seeming imaginability *versus*, 49–51, 52n.15, 53, 58, 114
real man
  primal answer of, 116–123
  primal question of, 115–116
  primality of, xviii, 60–61, 66, 71, 76–80, 96–97, 111
real possibility-imaginability, 49–51
real possibility projection, 10–13, 12n.3, 13n.4, 39
reality
  conceivability of, 21–23
  necessary connections and, 52n.15
  in real distinction, 12–13, 12n.3
reality-bound representations, of pain, 47–48
reality-projection principle, 21–22

INDEX

reflection principle, of reality, 22–24
representations, in de dicto premise, 49, 56n.18
rigid designators, in pain distinction, 45, 49

scientific discoveries, whatness of, 39–40
seeming conceivability, real conceivability *versus*, 19, 62, 66n.1
seeming imaginability, real imaginability *versus*, 49–51, 52n.15, 53, 58, 114
self-sufficiency, of human being, 60
semantic theory, in real distinction, 4
sensations, in real distinction, 56, 81n.9
separability
　conceivable, 5, 59, 101, 103–104
　existential (*see* existential separability)
　of mind and body, xvii–xviii, 5–8
　modal, 59–60, 107
　nature, 101
　in whatness, 5, 7, 59–60, 99
separatist dualism
　attributes in, 62–63, 67–68
　of body-in-general, 74–75, 80
　complete thing in, 66–68, 67n.2
　existential, 61–62
　generic, 62–64, 75
　generic essences of, 62–64, 75
　integrative dualism *versus*, 61, 71, 96n.15
　Meditation II on, 62–63, 65
　of mind, 79–81
　　divine, 62–63
　no endurance theory of, 63–66
　prove too much/prove too little dilemma of, 59–61, 66
　subject(s) in, 61, 65–66
　substance notion of, 59, 61, 66–69, 81n.9
set theory
　of integrative dualism, 110–111
　of mathematics, 34–36, 36n.13, 119
simpliciter, in real distinction, 70
soul, immortality of, 98n.16
species assertions, in primal answer, 120–123
stability principle
　failure of, 103
　as lifetime, 94–95
stages, in set theory, 35
subject(s)
　creation point of, 32–33, 33n.12
　extension to mind, 54–55
　imaginability of, 53–55
　lifetime description of, 65–66, 93–98
　real, complete, 59, 61, 66, 70, 99
　in separatist dualism, 61, 65
　whatness of, 28–29
subject-predicate structure, in imaginability, 53–54

subjecthood, complete, 59, 61, 66, 70
   existence apart and, 99–103
subjects in time, 81–98
   abstractionists challenge of, 91–93
   endurance of, 65–66, 85–91
   human mind as, 90–91
   lifetime principles of, 93–98
   Meditation II on, 82–83, 90
   metaphysics of, 83–84, 86–87
   piece-of-wax-as-a model of, 82–89, 114–115
   qualities of, 81–85, 82n.9
   separatist dualism of, 65–66
subspecies-aeternitate metaphysics, 83
substance
   bodies as
      generic, 75
      given kind, 77
   categorical conception of, 67–68, 77, 98, 100
   existence-free terms for, 67–69, 69n.4
   existential conception of, 67
   extension to mind, 54–55
   idea of, 3, 30–31
   of mind, 80
   modes of, 67–68
   predication of, 67–68, 79, 98
   real, complete, 59, 61, 66, 67n.2, 70, 99
   separatist ideas of, 59, 61, 66–69, 81n.9
subtraction principles
   necessity *versus*, 33–34
   of whatness, 8–10, 32–33
successor, in set theory, 35

symmetry
   in integrative dualism, 71–74, 80, 94n.13, 97
   of mind and body independence, 62–63

teletransporting devices, 112, 113n.5
thinking
   de re argument for, 56, 56n.18
   in whatness, 29, 31, 38–39, 58
thinking being, 106
thinking state, as phenomenon, 56–58
thinking thing, 38, 62
   stability of, 93, 95–96
thoughts, intuitions about identity of, 57
tight integrative dualism, generic *versus*, 109–112
transformation. *See also* change
   physical qualities of, 88–89
triangle. *See* geometry

universe of finite sets, 35–36

water
   conceivability of, 19–21
   imagining of, 50–51, 57
   as subject in time, 74, 83
   thinking of, 57–58
   whatness of, 27
wax-as-a model. *See* piece-of-wax-as-a model
wax passage, 85n.10
What am I?
   primal answer to, 116–123
   as primal question, 115–116

whatness
  Arnauld's notion of, 23–42
  of bodies, 77–78, 78n.8, 87
  coherent stories in quest for, 8–10, 38
  complete ideas in, 22–23, 29–33
  Descartes's notion of, 23–25, 28–29, 38–42
  epistemic, 24–27, 38–41
  essence of, 5, 52, 54, 64–65, 104
  exclusion in, 8–10, 30–33, 39
  extendedness of, 9, 15, 17, 38, 89
  ground facts of, 9, 26–29
  of mathematics, 27–28, 34–35, 37, 118–119
  metaphysical (*see* metaphysical whatness)
  necessity in, 28–29, 33–38, 40, 107n.2
  primacy of, 23–42
  in primal answer, 118–123
  priority over imagination, 54
  in real distinction, 5, 7–8
  robust, change and, 87–88, 90, 93, 93n.12
  subtraction principles of, 8–10, 32–33
  thinking states for, 29, 31, 38–39, 58
  too much *versus* too little in, 23–26, 33
whatness closure, 15
whatness-consistency, in man-mind swaps, 107–108
whatness facts, conceivability intuitions and, 104–107
whatness separability, 59–60, 99
whatness-specifying features, 28–29
wine, as item, 40, 43